Intuitive whisper: Now is the time
Rework your skills to help
and your ppl.

July 31, 29 Dragonflies(
- smell of Nature) pur~

The time is <u>now</u> to write my book

The Success Sense: Intuition for Entrepreneurs and Professionals

CANDICE M THOMAS

Copyright © 2016 Candice M Thomas

All rights reserved.

ISBN: 1523718056
ISBN-13: 978-1523718054

ACKNOWLEDGMENTS

I've been fortunate enough to be surrounded by people who helped me claim my inner 'woo-woo' while keeping me grounded in the world. There are so many who made a powerful impact in my life. Without them I would still be sitting in a cubicle waiting for my life to start.

I'd like to give acknowledgement to the people who had to 'suffer' through my writing process, my family and friends so close they're like family. You've seen me shine, you've seen me stumble, and you loved me anyway. Thank you Spirit, Thelma, Cal 3, Jack, Neil, Inga, Erica, and Mashell. I'm blessed to have you!.

CONTENTS

INTRODUCTION

Everyone is intuitive. There are many books and classes that teach how to understand intuition and the fundamentals of what it can be used for, but not many people talk about how to use intuition specifically for career and business success. This book aims to change that.

Your intuition is crucial to your success. Using intuition saves time, exposes you to greater opportunities, and helps you generate more income. With intuition you:
- Know right away if a job applicant would be a good fit for your company or if you are a good fit for a job
- Attract clients and customers who are a perfect for your services and products, customers who are *happy* to pay you for those products and services
- Understand the unspoken needs of your clients (or your boss) and know how to meet those needs to provide great service
- Easily make decisions about what to do next in your career
- Experience significant leaps in income
- Stop repeating the same cycles that leave you feeling

drained or stuck in your situation

These examples are just some of ways that intuition can be used. Many of my clients also experience unexplainable miracles where they attract opportunities such as being featured in national publications or getting large contracts from other companies "out-of-the-blue." In many of these situations my clients didn't seek these opportunities, people reached out to them. This is the brilliance of intuition. Intuition allows you to work in harmony with your divine power, your soul. When you are in alignment with your brilliance, success flows to you as opposed to you constantly trying to push and struggle to get your way. Think of how your life, not just your career, would change if you knew how to get all that you desired in the fastest and easiest way possible. This doesn't mean that you don't have to work. It means that you will work smarter, with intention, instead of working harder.

Speaking of "working hard," it's important to point out that using intuition is easy. It's easy to receive intuitive guidance and it's easy to understand. Ironically, because it is so easy, most people don't trust it! How many times have you heard that you have to work hard to get what you want? How many people do you know (including you) that *do* work hard but *aren't* getting what they want?

Not using your intuition leads to getting stuck, being indecisive about what next steps to take, and working from your pain rather than your brilliance. Working from pain means that you keep repeating the same patterns that frustrate you, such as having difficult coworkers or clients, being unable to move past a certain level of income, and/or constantly being burned out. Working from pain also causes entrepreneurs and employees to unknowingly turn down opportunities that would have skyrocketed their income. They might also give up on an idea only to see someone else do something similar and become famous overnight.

You may already be using your intuition to help your career

thrive. More than likely, you're not. Not because you aren't intuitive but because you:

- Aren't clear about what you truly want
- Don't recognize when your intuition is giving you information
- Don't understand what your intuition is telling you
- Confuse fear for intuitive guidance
- Aren't asking the right questions to receive the right answers
- Are so open to miscellaneous energy that you can't distinguish your true intuitive voice from the 'noise'
- Aren't doing what your intuition guides you to do

When you *actively use* your intuition you have the power to create the life you truly desire easily, right now. This book will show you how to use your intuition on purpose to get the results you want in an accelerated timeframe.

My Experience With Intuition and Success

I was born with strong intuitive abilities. I can see probable future events and connect with people who have died and crossed over into the spirit world. Even, though I was born with these abilities, I didn't know I had them! I didn't see dead people or hear spirits with my ears. Like many people my strongest ability is to *feel* intuitive information. I share this because many people don't recognize their intuition because what they do doesn't match what they see on TV or read in books.

I worked for the federal government for over 15 years as an accountant and financial analyst. Like I wrote above, I had no idea that I was intuitive. Even so, I was using my intuition most of the time on my job.

In the federal government are grade levels that signify your rank in the organization. The grade levels rank from GS-1 to GS-15. Beyond GS-15 are employees that are selected by congress. When I graduated college, I started with the federal government as a GS-9 accountant. I lived in Denver, Colorado but had to move to Laramie, Wyoming to accept the job. I was 21 at the time. I didn't want to stay in Wyoming or go back to Colorado; my goal was to move to Washington D.C. My close friends and coworkers were supportive of that idea even though there was no clear path to D.C. People outside of my close circle of friends encouraged me to just be happy where I was and be realistic about what I wanted. Competition was high in the agency, especially for jobs in D.C. According to them, it took *years* to get there and a GS-9 was pretty good. I ignored them. I wanted to go to D.C. and I knew I could get there. I couldn't explain to other people how I knew, I just *knew* I would do it even though there were no open jobs in that area and no clear path to get there.

I focused on learning as much as I could about accounting in my agency. I seemed to have a knack for getting mentored by the right people and choosing the right projects and assignments that increased my skillset. In a short amount of time, I was helping other people on the staff and getting involved in greater projects. I thrived. After a year and nine months, a coworker asked if I had seen a job advertisement for a position in Washington D.C. The job was for a financial analyst that had a series of guaranteed yearly promotions from a GS-9 to a GS-12. The application was due the next day! I applied for the job and based on recommendations from my supervisor, I was offered the position. In two years, I was moving to D.C. and was guaranteed to be a GS-12.

Reaction was swift and critical from people around me. Most told me to my face that I was "lucky." Others were baffled and assumed that there was some secret conspiracy to hire young people or black people or both. It wasn't luck that got me a promotion—I consistently worked to do my best. I also *actively used* my intuition to hold the space for what I wanted to experience even though I didn't consciously know that's what I had done!

By "hold the space" I mean that I created a specific and clear intention of "I am going to D.C. quickly" and then I took consistent action. This created a gateway of energy that pulled in the right people, situations, and circumstances that manifested my intention.

At some point in their lives, most highly intuitive people have had the experience of being able to get almost anything—all they had to do was think about what they wanted and it would manifest for them. However, for many people this ability doesn't last or it comes and goes. This happens when they inadvertently switch to manifesting from their pain versus their brilliance.

For me, my ability to manifest seemingly shut down when I applied for a new job and was promoted to a GS-13 supervisory financial analyst. I had been with the agency for eight years by then. I was one of the youngest GS-13's in my agency at 27. I supervised employees who were at grades GS-9 and lower. Even though I was a supervisor, I was also responsible for analyzing data for accounts ranging from hundreds to multimillions of dollars. This was a very demanding and high stress job; we were understaffed but still expected to meet critical deadlines. No excuses allowed. This was very hard on my supervisor and all of our staff. Many of us were convinced that our situation sucked and there was nothing we could do.

During this time, I started to feel like my body was filled with sand; I was exhausted and overwhelmed most of the time. I was also aware that I could *feel* the energy of the people around me. If they were irritated or upset, I would get sick to my stomach.

Because what was happening to me was weird I didn't tell many people. I worked up enough courage to see an intuitive. She told me that I was intuitive too. I was skeptical but I took her advice and began going to meditation classes and taking different workshops. By doing so, I found myself in the 'woo-woo' world of spirituality. I discovered mentors and teachers who I strongly resonated with and from them learned hypnotherapy, life and business coaching, channeling, and mediumship.

By day I was a mild mannered accountant working for the

government but by night I was a woo-woo intuitive reader. I began using what I had learned in the woo-woo world and brought my intuitive skills into my day job.

I wasn't giving readings; instead I was quietly "holding the space" for my staff and our coworkers. Instead of believing that our situation sucked and there was nothing we could do, I focused on what I wanted to experience and took responsibility for my happiness. This meant I couldn't blame other people for how I felt. I began 'seeing' the energy of the people around me and was able to block people from draining me. Gradually, over two years, things became much easier on the job.

At work I noticed that the people around me were also intuitive! Accountants, financial analysts, HR staff, it didn't matter. We were *all* sending out energy and receiving it from each other.

Outside of my government job I taught workshops to show others how to use their abilities in a practical way. I attracted entrepreneurs and business professionals who were looking for how to use their intuition to thrive in their career. As I worked with my clients by giving them intuitive tools and helping them hold the space for what they wanted, they experienced dramatic changes in their businesses. I've had clients who shifted from nearly shutting down their business to generating significant income, clients who created innovative products and services that attracted national attention, and clients who even used the intuitive tools they learned to heal personal relationships with loved ones in their lives.

After seeing so many clients get phenomenal results, I left my government job and began working full time as an intuitive coach.

Fate, Destiny, and the Power of Intuition

In the very early days of my intuitive career before I was an intuitive coach, I gave 'fortuneteller' readings, meaning, a person would ask a question along the lines of "what will happen to me?" and I would tell them what I 'saw' in their future.

During one of these readings I met a client who only had one question: was she going to marry her current boyfriend. I saw two different outcomes: one where she did marry her boyfriend and one where she didn't. I told her what I was seeing. As I spoke, I started getting clear information about the *energy* of both outcomes. I could see the energy of her emotions and limiting beliefs that were leading to an outcome of 'no marriage' and I could see the energy of the emotions that would have to be nurtured and the actions my client could take to manifest marriage.

My world changed in that moment. It became very clear that the purpose of being intuitive is less about predicting the future and more about creating it.

Instead of "Will this happen to me?" the question we should ask is "How do I make this happen?"

Some people aren't even sure of what they want. They come to me asking what they should be doing as a career or what to implement in their business. I hear variations of "what does God want me to do? What's my soul purpose?"

I have consistently seen that what my clients wanted the most was exactly what their soul came to earth to experience. Their soul purpose was the 'thing' that they had always dreamed about doing no matter how unrealistic it seemed. When I focused intuitive readings on how my client could achieve what they wanted instead of if they could have it, we strongly connected and received guidance from their soul and the collective conscious of the Divine.

Often times when my clients received that guidance they would tell me something along the lines of, "I thought about doing that" or "that's so odd, I was going to do that but changed my mind." This was evidence that my clients were getting intuitive information directly for themselves. When my clients took the actions their soul guided them to take they saw the results they wanted.

The more that I work with people the more I clearly see that yes, we *all* have the ability to create whatever we want to experience in our lives right now. If you truly have the desire to be world leader, have a billion dollar company, or even be famous, it is possible for you to achieve that. In fact, if you keep dreaming about achieving that level of success you are getting a nudge from your soul that you're *supposed* to be going in that direction. Our soul purpose will keep filtering up through our thoughts, influencing our deepest dreams and desires. Our intuition gives us the ability to manifest those dreams into reality.

Who This Book Will Help

My clients are in a variety of industries including general contracting, design, health and beauty, art, and more. While my clients come from a variety of backgrounds and are in different industries, they *all* have a

1. Strong belief that there is a great spiritual force in the world and that they are part of that energy
2. Strong belief that they are meant to be doing what they are passionate about as a career and are unwilling to settle for less
3. Genuine desire to provide the best possible products and services to inspire and uplift as many people as they can through their work and
4. Genuine desire to be extremely successful

When I write "extremely successful," I mean my clients have the desire to generate significant income, expand their business operations across the United States or all over the world, and become innovative leaders in their industry. It's not necessary for them to know exactly how they will do this, it is more important that they *believe* that they can. If you share these beliefs, this book will help you.

If you don't believe that you have the power to create what you desire or if you don't feel that you're supposed to make money doing what you love or if you just want to get rich without being of service to others then the concepts in this book will be very challenging. This doesn't mean that you're wrong for what you believe; it just means that this may not be the book for you.

This book gives special attention to entrepreneurs but anyone can use these concepts to help in their career. While there may be some general information on attracting clients and setting up the right products or services, this book does not go into detail about how to start and run a business. The focus will be on how to use your intuition to manifest career success.

How To Get The Most Out Of This Book

Be sure to read chapters 1 - 3, which are the essential intuitive tools that you need to manifest the success you desire. Chapters 4 – 9 focus on different subtle energies related to career and business success and don't need to be read in order. Where concepts are linked together across multiple chapters, there will be notes about where additional information can be found in the book. As you read through the chapters, take time to answer any questions asked—especially if the subject is an area where you are having challenges. Chapters 11 - 13 contain guided meditations and breathing exercises that will help you get your own intuitive guidance.

While reading different sections you may find yourself upset or irritated with what I've written. If that happens, hooray, your stuff is coming up! Often times people get the most triggered before they shift into a different mindset that will change them for the better. That being said, as you read this book please honor your true feelings: take what resonates with you and leave the rest behind.

You'll see me use the word "intuition" almost everywhere as opposed to using words like "psychic" or "medium". Psychic and psychic mediumship abilities are different facets of intuition. Because this book is geared toward entrepreneurs and business professionals I have kept things simple by using one term.

Where I write about other people, I have minor details to maintain confidentiality. However, the events are real.

The universes always sins to what we call for

CHAPTER 1
IT'S AN ENERGY GAME

The universe always gives us what we ask for. If you are experiencing something you don't like such as feeling stagnant in your career, struggling to get clients, or being broke, there is something within you that is *choosing* that outcome.

The world around us always mirrors our inner *vibration*, the energy of our spirit, thoughts, feelings, and emotions. There are two types of energies that flow in our vibration—the energy from our divine brilliance and the energy from our pain. We direct our intentions through one or the other! Depending on what we choose, we will experience two completely different outcomes even if we take the exact same actions. This is an important concept: your energy is often times more important than the actions you take. You can change the level of success that you experience by choosing the energy you operate from.

If you operate from the vibration of your pain while taking action you may manifest more hardship than success. This is why some people who work hard never get what they desire while other people seem skyrocket to the top of their industry in a short amount of time. It's not luck or fate or destiny that causes this.

It's energy!

This is why it's important to understand when you are manifesting from pain versus brilliance.

Pain

Most people aren't consciously thinking, "I'd like my life to suck right now," this choice is being made for them by the limiting beliefs in their subconscious. When you were a child your subconscious mind looked at all of the experiences you were having and came up with a reason for *why* you were experiencing them. Your mind's reasons for why things happened to you in the past became rules for how *everything* will happen to you in the present and future. When a rule is created out of a painful experience it becomes a subconscious limiting belief. That limiting belief constantly runs in the background of your thoughts and emotions, influencing your actions and how you view the world.

For example, a girl who grew up in a home where her family always struggled to make money may pick up the subconscious limiting belief *"It's hard to make money."* This belief will stay with her into adulthood.

As an entrepreneur, if she meets a potential client who really wants to pay for her services, she may feel uncomfortable or uneasy around that person. On an intuitive level she would sense her client would easily pay her. Her subconscious mind would realize that the potential client's desire to pay doesn't match the belief system *"it's hard to make money."* Not wanting to break it's own rule, the entrepreneur's subconscious mind would influence her to take actions to disrupt the sale. This means the entrepreneur would do things like show up late to meetings, choose not to work with the potential client, ignore the potential client altogether, or worse. The entrepreneur's subconscious isn't trying to hurt her; it's only trying to maintain the rule *"it's hard to make money."*

Conversely if the entrepreneur met a potential client who had a subconscious limiting belief of "*I shouldn't have to pay for anything*" on an intuitive level the entrepreneur would sense the potential client's unwillingness to pay. Her subconscious mind would say, "*It's hard for me to make money*" and her potential client's subconscious would answer, "*great, because I don't want to pay you!*" This might cause the entrepreneur to have a strong emotional resonance with the other person's limiting beliefs. The entrepreneur's subconscious limiting beliefs would influence her to do whatever she could to work with the person, such as lowering prices, offering to do more work for the same price, or allowing the person to overstep boundaries. Later on, her client might be resistant to paying or ultimately default on a bill.

The entrepreneur's intuition would have originally given her a knowing that "this person will not pay you" but the entrepreneur's emotions would have strongly influenced her to work with the client anyway.

This happens all the time. Everyone has an intricate series of hidden rules running in their energy that attract people and circumstances that match their belief system. Every person is intuitive enough to recognize the pain that is operating in another person's energy. This is why people may find themselves instantly attracted to people, careers, or situations that aren't really in their highest and best interest. They recognize the energy of the other person or situation and emotionally resonate with the pain they know they'll experience with that person or situation.

Who's Pain Is It Anyway?

If you constantly struggle with self-esteem, hopelessness, or other negative emotions, please realize that most of those feelings aren't actually yours; you're carrying what someone else gave you! Most of the pain you are experiencing is not generated from inside you but gets sucked into your energy field and trapped there. This toxic energy comes from other people's negative thoughts and feelings. It is also possible to have energy from your ancestral lineage stick to you. This is why certain families seem to experience the same kinds of problems generation after generation.

Negative energy you've taken from others is usually so subtle you don't notice, but that energy shapes your behavior.

For years I would talk negatively, calling myself "stupid" and chastising myself whenever I made a mistake. One day I realized, "I sound just like my dad." The reason I sounded like him was because I was carrying his old energy! My dad would say those things to me all the time when I was younger. The energy of his words had linked into my vibration. In my adult life I never felt good enough--even when I was getting accolades and praise from others, even when I was moving up the ladder in my government job at an accelerated rate there was a part of me that always felt like I was stupid. This feeling held me back from pursuing my true dream of being my own boss. When I recognized that I was carrying someone else's truth, I surrendered that energy and disconnected from it. Suddenly I was no longer feeling like I was stupid.

Activity

When you feel fear, doubt, worry, or other negativity surrender it. Surrender just means that you are consciously letting go of that energy. To do this, say, "I surrender [whatever negative emotion or thought you're feeling]. Spirit take this energy right now." Be sure to use the exact words that are coming up for you in that moment. For example, "I surrender feeling stupid. Spirit take this energy right now" or even "I surrender feeling scared shitless. Spirit take this energy right now."

Surrender is a powerful exercise because you don't have to fix your feelings or think positive. You are surrendering to the will of Spirit, your divine brilliance.

The more that you are consciously aware of what's happening in your thoughts and how you are feeling, the easier it will be to actually 'see' the pain you're carrying. Once you see it, it becomes less powerful. You will also be able to stop other harmful energy from attaching to you in the first place and clear anything that has connected with you. This is another way in which intuition is powerful: when you trust and follow your intuition, you connect to the powerful healing of your brilliance.

Your Brilliance

Each person on earth is a soul being with a unique mission. This mission is what the soul wants to learn and experience. It's the big 'why' a person has been born.

Your secret desires, the dreams that keep popping up in your mind over and over again are guides from your soul about what you're supposed to be doing. When in doubt, you only have to ask, "What do I *really* want to do?" When you do work that makes you happy, inspires you, or uplifts you, you are fulfilling your soul mission.

Only part of your soul comes down to earth and connects to your physical body, the rest of your soul remains in the spirit world as a higher consciousness of energy. This part of you is your 'higher self.' Your higher self knows exactly what you came to earth to do. Your higher self wants you to successfully complete your mission. Your higher self knows what's in your highest and best interest and is constantly giving you insights about what to do next to manifest your goals. This is why information you receive through your intuition is *always* accurate.

Through your higher self you are also connected to a greater energy, a Divine Intelligence that supports you in everything that you do. Tuning into the Divine Intelligence is like tapping into an infinite collective consciousness. This consciousness knows everything, it understands everything, and it loves you unconditionally. Some people refer to this as Source, God or Goddess. I use the term "Spirit". Everything is part of Spirit. Your brilliance is Spirit. Your angels are Spirit. Your loved ones in heaven are Spirit. You are Spirit.

When you use your intuition to tune into Spirit you step out of the limitations of the pain you've been carrying and tune into solutions and miracles of the universe. You only have to ask Spirit for guidance and you will receive answers.

Ask

Where Are You Manifesting From?

From moment to moment we are all making the choice to manifest our reality from our pain or from our brilliance. We get information from our intuition and our subconscious limiting beliefs all the time. Your life can dramatically improve just by being present and aware of where you are manifesting from when you make decisions.

Ask

When you have thoughts and feelings about what you want to do next ask, "is this coming from my pain or my brilliance?" Most people will get a knowing right away. You can ask this question when you are feeling fearful or skeptical or unsure. Trust your first impression when you feel like you have an answer. Do your best to operate from our brilliance, even when it feels uncomfortable or outright scary. Every time you recognize the difference between manifesting your soul truth versus your pain, the intensity of your limiting beliefs will lessen and your intuitive brilliance gets stronger.

CHAPTER 2
INTUITION 101

The way to connect with your divine brilliance is to actively use your intuition. Intuition allows you to recognize and understand energy.

Everything is energy: our bodies, thoughts, emotions, businesses, cars, houses, and anything else we can think of. These energies are constantly vibrating. Energies that vibrate at a faster rate or higher frequency may be harder for some to perceive than energies that vibrate at a lower speed or frequency. For example, our bodies vibrate at lower speed so we can see and touch and feel each other. Our emotions vibrate at a higher speed that most people may not pick up on if they're not familiar with their own intuition.

Your energy is contained within a magnetic field that surrounds and flows through your physical body. This field, called an aura, contains the energy of your thoughts, emotions, and experiences. Through your auric field, you can tune in and 'read' another person's energy or the energy of places, objects, and situations. This is how you are instantly drawn to people who end up reminding you of your parents or your ex—your energy

7

recognizes their energy.

"Energy" is just another word for information. Intuition allows us to tune into the information around us—we can 'look' into the energy field of another person, place, or situation and get information about what their goal truly is, if they're really in our highest and best interest, and what will most likely happen in the future to them (and to us if we choose to associate with them). Within the first few seconds of meeting a person or hearing an idea, we get impressions of this information. This is why most people say to "trust your first impression." The information transfer happens so quickly that your mind can't rationalize or minimize what you received.

Intuition is your link to Spirit. As written in the previous chapter, Spirit is a divine intelligence that has all of the answers and resources to help you move forward on your path. It is important that you actively partner with Spirit in all that you do.

Spirit Helpers

Some of my clients and students are used to asking specific spirit beings for help such as spirit guides, angels, ascended masters, and more. One of the greatest spiritual energies that is often overlooked is the energy of our own soul. When I am intuitively guided to give action steps to clients, the actions that give them the most phenomenal results are often from their higher self. Remember *you* are Spirit. To access all of your miracles you have to honor yourself as a divine being that has all the connections you need.

It is absolutely okay to ask specific beings like angels or spirit guides to assist you. Certain exercises in this book will ask you to invite them. Here is a brief description of the different spirit helpers that assist us and how they help. This list is not all-inclusive; I only included the energies that I work with the most for career success:

    1. Angels/Archangels – very strong healing energies, they won't interfere (aka help) in our lives unless asked. The reason is that they don't want to get in the way of our free will. To get assistance from angles, ask them for help. Messages from angels are usually broad loving statements (i.e., trust yourself, it will all be alright). They also bring through loving and healing energy that can be felt.

2. **Spirit Guides** – Beings that are with us 100% of the time. We don't need to ask them for help, they agreed to help us before we incarnated on earth. They are very easy to understand and for most people sound similar to the voice in our head. They don't make decisions for us; they give us insights and help guide us on our journey. They can strengthen connections to Spirit energy and call in angels/archangels and other beings for extra support if needed.

3. **Ascended Masters** – Believed to be humans who ascended and are now helping humans on earth to do the same thing; Jesus Christ and Buddha are examples. Like angels they give high healing energy. Their healing energy affects us on subtle but powerful levels. They also give guidance; their message is usually about partnering with Spirit and honoring the master within. Their messages tend to focus on the "big picture" as opposed to specific action steps.

4. **Higher Self** – The divine aspect of our specific identity and personality that can see exactly what we came on earth to do and works with other Spirit energies to make sure that happens. This aspect also gives detailed actions to take to manifest what we desire in the highest and best way.

5. **Soul** – Our entire consciousness beyond our singular expression. This is the real us, which includes our past life/present/future lives all at once and is perfect.

I advise my clients to ask for the highest and the best beings to assist them—this way, they don't get caught up in the 'rules' about which being to ask for what service. I learned early on in my intuitive career that these different forms of Spirit work together to help clients succeed. This is why I use the term "Spirit"; it's easier than naming all of the beings who are here to help!

Understand Your Intuition

You receive information from all around you (and from Spirit) through your aura. When your energy field perceives that information, your brain translates the energy into something that you recognize—a physical feeling, a knowing, a sound, an image, or even a smell or taste. This is why intuition is so subjective—our brains process information in different ways.

This doesn't always mean that you understand what you're receiving. The more present that you are the better you'll be able to understand your intuition. Being present means being aware of how you're feeling and what you're observing around you. The breathing exercise *Check In* located in chapter 11 will help you be more present. If you allow yourself to observe what you are experiencing without judgment you will notice that you're actually getting many intuitive insights throughout the day in a variety of ways. You may:

1. **Feel Energy - *You receive sensations in your physical body or in your emotions ("trust your gut," "I have a funny feeling," etc.)***

   Feeling energy is called clairsentience. This feeling occurs in the physical body and can sometimes affect emotions as well. What a person feels will vary. Buzzing, tingling, spasms, temperature changes, and sudden emotional shifts are examples of how your sense of feeling may be affected. Your body is giving you intuitive information all of the time. This means whenever you're meeting someone or taking an action, making a decision, or even watching a movie, your body is giving you guidance about what you're experiencing, specifically 'telling' you if that person, situation, decision, etc. is in your best interest or not. Generally speaking, if your body feels good around people or in situations, it's a sign that "yes" it's okay for you. If your body feels bad it's a sign that "no" it's not okay for you. By feeling bad I mean you may experience actual aches and pains, tension or tightness. The physical feeling may be different than your emotional feeling. Some sensations don't feel good or bad at all, just different. When you are aware of a new feeling, sensation or if your mood suddenly shifts, tune in and ask yourself:

- "Is this from me or somewhere else?"
- "Where is this in my body? And what is it connected to?"

You will receive additional insights about the energy. The insights may be a knowing or an image or a thought—trust your first impression. The more that you practice tuning into how you feel in your body, the more specific your impressions will be. For example, for a long time I felt fear whenever I was faced with decisions in my business. I started tuning into the emotion and noticed that I felt the fear in different places in my physical body. If I felt fear on the back of my neck and shoulders it meant that the fear was irrational, from my own mind; if I felt fear in the pit of my stomach I knew that the fear was a warning from my intuition that the situation, person, or decision connected to that feeling was not in my highest and best interest.

As written in the previous chapter, it is possible to take on energy from other people without being consciously aware of it, especially their pain. The feeling that many people experience when this happens is irritation. If other people or situations constantly irritate you, it is a sign you are being overwhelmed by the energy of the people and situations in your life. Other common physical feelings when negative energy connects with you include having a sensation like something is being pulled or pushed in your stomach area, sharp jabbing pains (like feeling stabbed in the back), and suddenly feeling tired or sluggish.

If you experience these sensations, tune in to what's connecting with you. By asking the question "is this me or someone else" you can instantly identify energy that is not yours entering your vibration. The moment you recognize it's not yours the energy will begin to disconnect. You can completely disconnect from the energy by saying silently or out loud "leave my energy right now." Those don't have to be your exact words. Even saying something like "cancel clear" or "no thank you" is powerful enough to break the connection. When the connection is broken, the pain or irritation will stop.

To better understand your intuition, practice feeling it. Throughout the day check in with yourself and notice what you are feeling in your physical body. Notice how your body feels when you're taking actions for your business or in your job. Notice how those feeling change depending on who you interact with. As you do this, you will recognize the subtle impressions you're receiving from your intuition.

2. **Hear Energy – *You hear energy with your ears or in your thoughts ("Something said to..." "A thought popped in my mind to...")***

Spirit speaks to us in a way that we can hear; this is called clairaudience. It is possible to hear with your ears— you may hear voices or sounds like a high-pitched or low-pitched tone that you can't explain. More people hear Spirit in their thoughts. The voice that speaks in your head and sounds like you may actually be a message from Spirit. Songs that come to mind for no reason or memories of what you heard are also forms of hearing energy. Spirit is usually succinct and to the point. For example, if you're going through a crisis and you ask "am I going to be okay?" You might only hear "yes."

Hearing energy can be hard to trust if you are 'hearing' your own voice—you might think you're hearing your own thoughts, not your intuition. A great exercise that I learned from medium John Holland is to ask, "is this from me or to me?" when you aren't sure where a message is coming from. Another way to ask that question is "is this me or Spirit?" After you ask that question trust your first impression. This will help you decipher what is a true Spirit message and what's not.

Some people will feel a buzzing, tingling, or other sensation on the back of their neck when they get clairaudient messages. Even if you don't get this sensation, the way to know the difference between hearing Spirit guidance and your thoughts is to be as mindful as you can, paying attention to what you perceive. Over time you will notice thoughts from Spirit sound slightly different than your own thoughts.

Hearing energy is associated with the throat. Some people store other people's energy in their throat area. If you have coughing fits from out of nowhere or constantly struggle to clear your throat you may be experiencing other energy connecting with you. Ask the question, "is this from me or someone else?" Trust what you receive. As written before, the moment you identify that the energy doesn't belong to you, it begins to disconnect.

Psychic mediums who have the ability to get messages from people who have died and gone on to the afterlife may frequently have coughing fits that they can't explain or hear seemingly random messages in their minds that they don't understand. If this is your experience, please be sure to look at chapter 9 in the *Healing Tools For Empaths* section for tools to help you through your unique challenges.

3. **See Energy – *You see energy with your eyes or in your mind's eye ("I saw that coming")***

There are people who can see energy with their eyes. This means they can perceive auras or even see spirit beings and more. There are many people who see energy in their thoughts. Both ways of seeing energy are called clairvoyance. Spirit will use what you know and what you've already seen as a library of reference. This means when you ask Spirit a question, an image of something that you saw before may pop up in your thoughts. You may see many images that appear almost all at once, like watching a movie; or you may see one image. For most who see energy in their thoughts, the images appear very briefly and disappear. It is easy to miss or forget what you see if you aren't paying attention to what's coming into your awareness.

Spirit has the power to focus your vision on certain people or objects. This means you may find yourself really staring at something that stands out to you in a big way. There's no logical reason why it stands out. When this happens, be observant of what you feel and what you may be hearing in your thoughts. You may also get a knowing around why what you're looking at is important. For example, I was looking through an old client list when one name on the list suddenly stood out to me. When I saw the person's name, I felt compelled to reach out to them. When I called my former client they said that it was a miracle I'd called—they really needed a session with me.

Like above if you're ever unsure of whether your imagination or your intuition has given you a clairvoyant message, ask the question "is this me or Spirit?" Trust your first impression.

To increase your ability to see energy you have to pay attention to what you see with your eyes. You also have to notice when images are coming into your mental awareness. It is also important to visualize what you want to experience. Any time you use your imagination to 'see' an image in your thoughts you are strengthening your clairvoyance.

4. Know Energy – *You have a strong knowing* ("*I knew it!*")

Just knowing information can be one of the hardest intuitive abilities to recognize and trust. There's no logical reason why you know it, you just do. This is called claircognizance. A strong knowing usually comes with a very strong feeling that the information is right. A person with this ability is good at solving problems and seeing the 'big picture'—the answers just come to them. People with this ability can be extremely analytical. If you ask them *how* they know what they do they usually say something like, "it's common sense." They can't believe that no one else sees the same solution; to them it's *obvious*.

When I was a financial analyst my boss asked me to come up with a solution to migrate data between financial systems. Just as I was saying, "I don't know how" I received an instant knowing of how to do it—I knew the software to use, formulas to enter, and more. The knowing came from out of nowhere. I trusted my new knowledge and came up with a solution, then helped implement the project.

Knowing energy can mean that you know all of the intricate details or you may only know one specific piece of information. For example, you may instantly know if planned event will be a success or a failure but you don't know *why*.

When you get a download of knowledge from Spirit, you don't have to think about it. The information easily comes to you. When it comes to you, it feels right.

Some people experience a sensation of feeling tingling or buzzing at the top of their heads or they may even have the sensation that their head is somehow opening up as they receive a download of knowledge from Spirit.

To strengthen this ability, get into the habit of asking Spirit for knowledge or asking for a solution to specific problems you may be experiencing. When you ask, pay attention to what drops into your knowing. Having clear thoughts instead of constant mental chatter will help develop this ability. Meditation is a powerful way to clear your mind. Like above if you're ever unclear whether a thought is from your intuition or if you've made it up, ask the question "is this me or Spirit?" You will receive an answer that will help you separate true intuitive knowing from your own thinking.

5. **Taste and Smell Energy**

Clairgustation and Clairolfactory are the abilities of intuitively tasting and smelling energy. Tasting and smelling energy can work in a variety of ways. Many people experience this when they are getting messages from their loved ones in the afterlife. For example, if your grandfather smoked a special brand of cigar, after he passes away you may suddenly smell that unique cigar smoke for no logical reason. If he liked to eat a certain food, you may suddenly taste that food even if you aren't eating anything.

These are two fun senses to play with. To develop your strengths in these areas, just ask Spirit to give you information in a way you can taste or smell. You can even go to a grocery store and practice tuning into different foods or produce to see if you get a 'hit' on what would taste good or not.

There is much more information about each of these intuitive abilities and how to strengthen them. The best way to develop your intuition is to use it on purpose. Take a workshop or class where you can practice these abilities with other like-minded people. It is also a good idea to read books from different authors about intuitive development. I highly recommend that you start with the book *Psychic Intelligence* by Terry and Linda Jamison.

The Softer Voice

Intuitive information comes very quickly and can be very subtle. Most people won't receive overwhelming physical sensations or hear a loud voice in their mind. Instead, they may get a brief feeling or a fleeting thought that's gone almost before its recognized. This can make it easy to dismiss intuition.

I've had clients who experienced a moment of intuitive gold—one time in their life where they had a very clear, amazing intuitive experience. They thought that these moments were the only time their intuition worked. They didn't realize that their intuition was working perfectly all along. Your intuition doesn't need to beat you over the head to give you a strong message. Even if the message is subtle you will still understand it if you're present enough to recognize it.

When you first recognize your intuition, the information you receive may seem vague. For example, you may get a sudden uncomfortable feeling when you think about a current project you're involved in. If that feeling was the only intuitive impression you received, you may not understand why you feel that way or what your intuition is really trying to tell you. When you have an initial intuitive hit, you can use that impression to get more specific information from Spirit. You do this by asking specific questions along the lines of who/what/when/where/how/why. In the above example, if you suddenly had an uncomfortable feeling about a project, you could ask, "What area of the project is this discomfort connected to? (Other people, the work itself, financing, etc.)" You could also ask, "What's in my highest and best interest to do in this situation?"

You will receive more insight as you ask the right questions and stay present with what you receive. Trust your first impression.

While most people experience intuition in a subtle way, there are other people who are overwhelmed by it. They constantly absorb energy from other people or receive messages from beings in Spirit that aren't always in their highest and best interest. If you can relate to this be sure to check out the *Healing Tools For Empaths* section in chapter 9 and do the *Check In* breathing exercise in chapter 11. Both have techniques you can use to clear and protect your energy.

Intuition vs Imagination

Many students that I teach in my intuitive workshops don't have problems connecting with Spirit and getting messages. They have more trouble *trusting* what Spirit is guiding them to do. They are worried that what they perceive is just their imagination. Here are some ways to tell the difference between your intuition and imagination:

1. **Intuition is the First Voice (Your Mind is the Second)**

   Your thoughts and emotions can seem 'louder' than your intuition. In most cases, the first impression you receive or the very first thought you have is your intuition giving you guidance. It occurs in less than a split second. Immediately after you get an intuitive hit your brain may doubt the guidance and give you a feeling of fear or confusion. When in doubt about a message you received, ask 'is this coming from me or Spirit?' Trust your first impression. If it's coming from you, it may be tied to a subconscious limiting belief that is the opposite of what your intuition says.

2. **Intuition Feels Different**

   If you are fully present and aware of how you're feeling when you receive information from Spirit you will notice that the messages from your own thoughts come attached with an emotion. Intuitive guidance doesn't often have an emotional feeling attached, positive or negative. In fact, feelings of being super excited while you are receiving a message usually point to out-of-balance emotional energies. The exception to this is that some messages come with a profound feeling of love and peace.

3. **The Same Intuitive Message Comes In A Variety Of Ways**

   Intuitive guidance doesn't come in just one way to a person. You may see an image, get a knowing, and a feeling all at once. Your intuition will also use what you already know to convey messages—if you ask for guidance about a specific issue you may suddenly recall a scene from a movie or see a friend's face and then get a feeling or a knowing about what that means.

4. **Intuitive Guidance Repeats**

   Intuition is the 'softer' voice but it also a nag. Spirit will repeat the same messages to you until you get it. If you continue to ignore your intuition, Spirit will connect to you through an outside source. For example, a friend will say something to you or you'll see something on television that resonates with you very strongly—that feeling is your intuition asking you to pay attention. It is possible for you to ignore your intuition to the point of missing out on opportunities. If that happens, Spirit will give you insights about new opportunities. Really take notice of what ideas keep coming to your mind that you're ignoring. What keeps showing up in your thoughts?

Help, My Intuition's Broken!

I have heard many variations of "I followed my intuition but it was wrong." When students tell me that their intuition was wrong they usually mean they experienced something they didn't like. There are several reasons why they might have had this experience. Remember, intuition is always right 100% of the time. Your intuition will always guide you toward what is in your highest and best interest. Sometimes what's in your highest and best interest isn't a happy experience.

The earlier example of an entrepreneur who has a subconscious limiting belief of "*it's hard to make money*" may get an intuitive hit to work with a client that ends up refusing to pay her for services. The experience may be just negative enough to convince the business owner to do the inner work that's necessary to get rid of that limiting belief. That situation may be the final straw that causes her to let go of what she thinks she knows and open up to the divine. This is how seemingly negative experiences such as a grief, heartache, and pain can help bring about greater healing and change in our lives.

Waiting too long to follow guidance from your intuition may result in you getting different results than what you would have gotten if you had taken action right away.

Finally, it is possible to fool yourself into thinking you're getting intuitive guidance when you're not. This goes back to the importance of being present and learning how to distinguish between your brilliance and your pain. Spirit will never shame, punish, or humiliate you. Spirit won't abandon you. If you're unclear about whether or not what you're receiving is really from Spirit, ask yourself "is this me or Spirit?" Trust your very first impression.

What Intuition Won't Do

If you don't understand a concept, intuition can't magically give you the understanding of that concept. For example, if you're not a brain surgeon you can ask Spirit to show you how to operate on a living brain and Spirit might download information to you but if you don't have a core competency in brain surgery, you won't understand what you are receiving. Some psychics are able to go so deep into the energy of Spirit that they can channel information in areas they aren't familiar with—this takes a high level of surrender and trust.

If you do ask Spirit for guidance in an area you don't understand, Spirit may lead you to a person who does understand it or a class where you can learn more. For example, if you ask Spirit for a marketing idea, you might get the urge to contact a branding expert or advertising company, someone who understands how to help you the most.

Intuition can't make your life better if you aren't willing to do the inner work and release the energy of your pain. This means taking responsibility for your happiness. If there is something you don't like in your situation, you must be brave enough to own your part in it instead of blaming others. If you feel like life is just happening to you, you won't be able to empower yourself to bring in greater success.

Intuition & Your Spirit Connection

I teach my clients to ask Spirit questions in their everyday life such as where to find a parking space or where to eat. The reason I have my clients do this is so that they build a stronger rapport with their higher self and get a better understanding of how they receive information from Spirit. It is easy to learn the language of Spirit when we aren't emotionally attached to the outcome.

I recommend that you do the same. Get into the habit of asking Spirit for suggestions or even tasking Spirit with doing things. For example, instead of asking Spirit "where is a good parking space?" you can task Spirit with "find me a good parking space."

This doesn't diminish Spirit or make spirit beings your servants. Spirit wants to partner with you. Whatever is on your heart to ask, ask. The *Ask Spirit For Guidance* section in chapter 4 will suggest specific questions to ask related to your career or business.

When you do get answers from Spirit, your mind may try to talk you out of believing it. The reason is that your thoughts are still restricted by your limiting beliefs. Your intuition doesn't play by the rules of your pain.   This means that what your intuition guides you to do will not make logical sense to your mind. Your mind will try to rationalize your intuitive experiences as coincidences or imagination. This is where believing that you have a soul purpose and you are meant to succeed in fulfilling that purpose becomes important. You have to have enough faith in yourself to ignore your pain and trust the brilliance of your intuition.

Seriously, Trust Your Intuition

It is very important to make the decision to trust yourself and your intuition right now. Too often people make the mistake of saying, "I'll trust my intuition when I know it's accurate."   The truth is that you won't get evidence of your intuition being accurate until you trust it first! If you wait for proof that your intuition is right before you take action, you will end up holding yourself back and missing opportunities. Putting pressure on yourself to be accurate also blocks the flow of information from Spirit. This is where taking an intuitive development workshop can help you get validation about what you're experiencing.

CHAPTER 3
FIVE STEPS TO MANIFEST SUCCESS

As an intuitive coach, Spirit guides me to go through the same steps with every client I meet. It doesn't matter how big my client's business is or what their career goals are, we go through the same steps. As my clients follow these steps many of them experience significant positive changes in a short period of time. One client went from having almost no clients to generating thousands of dollars and getting several clients in weeks. Another client's services were featured in *Vogue* magazine. Using the steps below, I walked away from my day job as a financial analyst in the government and started my own successful business.

The clients that have had great success didn't do anything dramatically different in their business to get these miracles. The business actions that they took week to week were mostly the same actions they had always been taking. It was their underlying *energy* that changed. Being more aligned with their soul truth opened a gateway for new opportunities. This goes back to the question asked in chapter 1: are you manifesting from your brilliance or from pain?

If you perform the five actions below consistently, you will stay in the brilliance of your divine spirit. The right people and opportunities will flow to you. The steps look so simple that you may want to skip them. Don't. If you find yourself getting irritated or if you feel resistant to doing these steps, that may be a sign that you're on the verge of a breakthrough and your subconscious mind is trying to stop you! If you do feel resistance to any of these steps ask yourself, "is this coming from my pain or my brilliance?"

The five steps to manifest success are to:

1. **Set Clear Intentions** - Be honest about what you want to experience, how successful you want to be, the impact you want to make, and why. This creates your divine vision.
2. **Connect With Spirit** – Meditate to connect to Spirit and sit in the vibration of your divine vision. Your old limiting beliefs and energetic blocks will loosen, allowing you to better understand your intuition.
3. **Ask Spirit For Guidance** – When you are in a higher state of consciousness, ask Spirit for the next steps to take to move forward in your business or for help with any situation. Spirit will respond with specific information to help you move forward in the highest and best way.
4. **Follow The Guidance From Spirit** - When Spirit tells you what action steps to take, take them. (This is the step that most people have trouble with.)
5. **Monitor Your Energy** - Every person will still experience the energy of their subconscious limiting beliefs, even if they follow their intuition 100%. Taking the same action from the energy of your pain will result in a completely different outcome than taking that action from your brilliance. Be mindful of where you're manifesting from and how to hold the space of your divine spirit.

Below is more detail about the steps individually. Read

through each of these steps carefully to get a better understanding of how to manifest.

1. Set Clear Intentions (Create Your Divine Vision)

Are you clear about what you want to give and receive? To have a successful business or career, your energy has to be focused and in alignment with what you truly desire. Not being clear about what you want to give and receive results in experiences such as feeling forced to provide services you dislike, attracting clients you can't stand, feeling stuck at a certain level of success, and/or continually investing in products or services that don't help you. This is true no matter what amount of money you're making.

Some people have a hard time deciding what they want. This usually occurs when a person *does* know what they want but they don't believe that they can get it. They try to think of alternatives to their true desires and end up feeling lost and disconnected.

Years ago, a client came to me for an intuitive reading, asking what he should do as a career. He had started a business that was barely paying expenses. He needed another job but he didn't know what to apply for; he had several different degrees but nothing seemed to interest him. What came through my intuition was that he was meant to be healing people. He was surprised when I said that. He told me he was a part time Reiki healer and *wished* he could that work full time but he hadn't been able to make money doing it. Spirit showed me very clearly that if he switched to doing his passion full time the money would follow. He was skeptical. Not many people he knew could support themselves doing that kind of work. He insisted I use my intuition to point him to a 'real' job. Spirit gave guidance for how he might improve his current business. Months after the reading, he contacted me to let me know that his business had failed but he was now doing his healing work full time. He was getting enough clients to support himself—he couldn't believe it. I told him that it happened because he was honoring his soul mission.

You came to earth on purpose. With a mission. Your mission wasn't to be small and fit in. Your purpose was to bring about healing and change through the work that you are passionate about. This means you have to have the courage to ignore what family or friends think is best for you and focus on what you really want to experience. Your wishes and desires are directions from your soul that tell you what you're meant to be doing in this life. If you've always dreamed of writing, you're meant to write. If you've secretly wished to be the head of a major corporation since you were a child then that is a sign that you're meant to go in that direction. It doesn't matter what you've experienced in the past or how far away your dream may seem. All that matters is that you be honest with yourself and get clear about what you want right now.

- What do you want to do in your career?
- Is that what you *really* want to do or are you making your goal fit with what you think you can have or what is expected of you?
- What do you want to feel and experience while doing your work?
- How many people do you want to reach? Who are they? How do you want to reach them?
- How much money do you want to make?
- Where do you want to live? What type of house and car do you want?
- Who do you want your partners and allies to be?
- Who do you want to share your success with?

These questions are a good starting point to help you set clear intentions. Notice what comes up for you as you answer those questions. You may find yourself wanting to 'check out' and skip over them without answering or you may suddenly be uncomfortable. That's a sign that you're bumping up against a limiting belief that's been holding you back from getting what you truly desire.

For now it's not necessary to worry about "how" it's possible for you to have what you want. It's also okay to be skeptical about whether or not you can manifest that desire. It's more important to be honest about what you want and *why* you want it.

The "why" has to be big enough for you to feel your divine brilliance. This means that as you think about what you really want and why that is important to you, you should *feel* a deep connection to your "why." If you don't really care about your work or if you're not convinced your work is important then you have a small "why". A small "why" manifests small results. To get in touch with your big "why" ask yourself:

- Why is doing your service(s) or providing your product important to you?
- How do your services change your clients' lives in a positive way? Why is that important to you?
- How do your services change the world in a positive way? Why is that important to you?
- What else do you feel called to do to inspire and lead others? Why is that important? How does that relate to your current career?
- What needs to change in your current career to match your big "why?"

In getting clear with your intention it is also important to be clear about what you want the energy of your business or organization to be. The energy of your business can be felt by everyone who comes into contact with you, your staff, your advertising, website, etc. What do you want others to perceive in your business or organization's vibration? Here are questions that can help you start focusing on that energy:

- What emotions do you want others to experience when they connect with your business? Why? Is that what your organization feels like to you right now?
- What do you want clients to feel after they receive products/services from you? Why?
- What kinds of customers/clients/partners do you wish to

27

work with?   What traits do you wish your clients, partners, and customers to have? Why?

- How does your business vibration match your divine 'why'?

I recommend writing down the answers to these questions and use those answers to create your intentions. An intention is a declaration. For example, if you desire to be a multibillionaire, your intention would be "I am a multibillionaire." Notice that the statement is written with "I am" instead of "I want." Also notice that the statement is written in present tense as if you're already a multibillionaire. When creating intentions it is important to write or speak them as if they are already happening right now.

It's also important that all of your intentions are positive and only focused on what you want to experience versus what you don't want to experience. For example, instead of saying, "I am not broke" or "I will stop struggling financially" powerful intentions would be "I am financially abundant right now" or "Right now I have more than enough money for everything."

You may have a hundred intentions or a just a few. Take the time to create them. Vision boards are other ways to get clear with intention—make sure that all aspects of what you intend are covered. For example, if you want things to be easy, include symbols or pictures that represent easiness.

As you encounter specific challenges in your business, you can focus on intentions for those specific issues, such as getting more clients or more income.

The more that you get clear with your intentions, the more that you start engaging Spirit to work with you and manifest those intentions into reality. All of your intentions create your divine vision. When you go into sacred space and feel the energy of your divine vision, you accelerate your ability to manifest your dreams.

2. Connect With Spirit

"Sacred space" is a term that describes an inner stillness

within you. This can be achieved through various forms of meditation, yoga, or even simple breathing exercises. When you are in sacred space, you consciously connect to your higher self and experience your divinity.

By closing your eyes and taking a few deep breaths you automatically shift into sacred space. You also begin to perceive the greater energy of Spirit. In this state, invite Spirit to step closer to connect with you. Simply saying, "Spirit, connect with me now" is enough. You may feel a lightness or heaviness, warmness or coolness, or even buzzing, trembling, or tingling sensations. You may also burp or yawn, which is a sign that you are releasing energy that's not in your highest and best interest.

It is best if you go into sacred space every day to connect with Spirit. Sitting in the stillness of your energy will help you release the vibration of pain and hold you in the energy of your brilliance.

When you are connected with Spirit, you can anchor the energy of your divine vision into your auric field. Like energy attracts like energy. By anchoring your intentions into your energy field, you attract opportunities and people that match the vibration of your intention. This is why it's important to set intentions for exactly what you want to experience.

To anchor your intentions in your auric field, read or recall your list of intentions. Imagine what it would be like if you had all of those things right now--the successful career you wanted, doing what you loved with your dream clients. Focus on what it would you would hear, and how you would feel. With the power of your imagination, allow yourself to experience your success as if it's already happening right now through your five senses. Imagine what emotions you would be feeling. Feel the gratitude and whatever other emotions you relate with.

When you are really feeling the energy, silently or out loud say, "Spirit anchor this vibration within my being right now. Dissolve and remove any energies that are not in alignment with my divine vision." Then be present with what you experience. A special guided meditation that will help you do this can be found in chapter 12.

After you become familiar with the feeling of your success you will be able to simply recall the feeling at any time of day whether you are meditating or not. This will only happen with continued practice. If you are new to energy work, I recommend going into sacred space with your intentions for at least 30 consecutive days.

3. Ask Spirit For Guidance

When you are feeling the energy of your intentions and divine vision, ask Spirit for guidance about what to do next. When you ask Spirit a question you will receive an answer. Example questions to ask Spirit when you're in sacred space include:

- What's in my highest and best interest to know right now?
- What's in my highest and best interest to release right now?
- Who do I call now to generate income?
- What project do I focus on first?
- What action do I take next?
- Should I choose (option 1) or (option 2)?

In the example questions above I am focusing on asking Spirit what to do right now or in the near future. This is because the power of your manifesting is in the now. If you ask Spirit a question like "what do I do?" Spirit may give you a more general answer. If you get specific by adding a timeframe, Spirit will get specific. If you ask Spirit a yes or no question, Spirit will answer you with a yes or no. If you're unsure of what to ask, a great question is "what's in my highest and best interest to know right now?"

No question is too big or too small for the Divine You. Your higher self wants you to succeed and will always give you answers that are accurate and in your highest and best interest.

Where do you struggle the most in your career? Ask Spirit "what's the most important thing for me to know right now regarding this situation." Write down what comes to mind. Trust your first impression. If you would like extra help and support with a specific challenge or situation, ask Spirit to assist you.

Sometimes the answers from Spirit come in a way that you weren't expecting or that you don't appreciate. For example, if you've asked Spirit to show you all the steps to become a millionaire and all they've done is show you this book, you might get frustrated. Spirit usually only gives you the information you need in the present moment. This means Spirit isn't going to show you all 10,000 steps you need to take to become a millionaire. However, the more you follow Spirit's guidance and take the action steps that are revealed to you, the easier it will be for Spirit to bring you more specific guidance about what to do next. This happens because as you take actions in alignment with your divine vision, you create more energy to manifest what you want.

As discussed in chapter 2, you may receive an answer from Spirit through a feeling, a knowing, an image, a sound, or a combination of all of the above. If you aren't used to asking direct questions then the responses you receive may seem very subtle.

You may think that you're not getting an answer from Spirit. This can happen if you expect to see or hear an answer when you're strongest intuitive ability is feeling or knowing information instead. If you feel like you have trouble understanding Spirit, reread chapter 2, especially the sections *Understand Your Intuition*, *The Softer Voice*, and *Intuition vs Imagination*. You might also consider taking an intuitive development workshop or studying books about developing intuition.

In addition to getting messages from Spirit, you can also receive assistance and healing energy. It is possible to ask Spirit for healing in a specific area of your life or business. You can also make requests of Spirit to help you or your business in specific

ways. For example:
- Please Spirit give me the energy I need to keep going
- Please Spirit, organize my schedule so everything falls into place easily right now
- Please Spirit, bring me my perfect employees easily right now
- Please Spirit, take away my confusion in this area completely right now

Like intentions, it is helpful to be clear with Spirit about what you want them to do. You can ask for help from specific beings such as angels or spirit guides or other beings you feel connected with. Some beings are better for certain areas of healing than others. This is why I usually say, "Spirit" instead of asking for a category of Spirit.

4. FOLLOW Guidance From Spirit

Your intuition operates from a big picture view. Your mind operates from the space of what it knows and the belief system it created. You slow down your ability to manifest when you don't take the actions your intuition guides you to take. The longer that you wait to take action, the more you risk losing an opportunity.

There will be times when what you plan and what Spirit guides you to do will be different. This is where people may not want to follow guidance from Spirit—the guidance may seem like it's in direct conflict with 'the plan.' Spirit knows what's in your highest and best interest. Trust the guidance you receive.

When you receive intuitive messages, trust your very *first* impression. Initially you may feel that the guidance is right and it feels good, then as your brain understands what your intuition is saying you may get a contradictory emotion. The emotions of pain are not your first impression but often feel stronger than what you initially received. This is why so many people don't take action on what their intuition guides them to do and why they agree to situations that aren't really in their highest and best interest. They are focused on their second impression, the negativity of their emotions.

Something that I see many people do is wait for when it "feels right" to take an action that would help their career, all the while they're missing out on opportunities. Being intuitive doesn't automatically erase your fear and doubt. As you take actions that bring success, you may feel very uncomfortable, especially if you're finally overcoming a subconscious limiting belief. If you get an intuitive hit and then suddenly feel like you're not ready to take action, ask yourself "is this coming from my pain or my brilliance?"

If you are truly unsure about when to take action, ask Spirit. "What do I do next?" or "Do I take action on this now or later?" are clear questions that help you get specific information about when to take action. Again, believe and trust the answer you receive.

Chapter 6 has more information about overcoming procrastination and getting out of the slow lane of manifesting.

5. Monitor Your Energy

The question that you'll see repeated throughout this book is an important one: are you operating from pain or your brilliance? Even if you take consistent actions based on the information you receive from Spirit, the way that you implement those actions may still be influenced by your subconscious limiting beliefs. This means that you can slip right back into manifesting from pain even when you follow the guidance from Spirit.

One of my clients had gotten an intuitive hit to join a special networking group. After a few weeks, he told me that he wanted to drop out of the group because he wasn't getting clients. I told him not to drop out. Instead we focused on his divine vision, what he wanted members of the group to experience, how he could support them, and why that was important. This shifted his focus to being of service instead of focusing on what he was getting out of the group. This brought him out of manifesting from pain and into alignment with his brilliance.

By our next appointment he had several people who were interested in working with him, one of those people became his first high-end client. The actions he took were mostly the same as before—he went to a networking event and networked. But because he was coming from a different energy, he was able to manifest exactly what he wanted instead of what his pain told him he could have.

When you aren't seeing the results that you would like or if you feel you are failing, you are seeing your subconscious limiting beliefs and the energy of the pain you're carrying.

When you experience setbacks and challenges you are experiencing that negative situation so you can finally shift out of the underlying pain that caused it. The closer you come to manifesting miracles in your life, the stronger your pain will come up. Stay strong when this happens. This means instead of saying things like, "nothing ever changes! I keep making the same mistakes! What's wrong with me?" say, "Hooray, my shit's coming up!" I advise my clients to say that phrase out loud when they encounter challenges. *"Hooray, my shit's coming up!"* stops the spiral of negative thoughts they are used to having when things don't go their way.

The more that you believe that you are stuck or that your situation is hopeless the more you will create that reality. No one is ever really stuck. The way to shift out of that feeling is to keep your energy grounded, cleared, and focused on the energy of your brilliance.

Keep Your Energy Clear

Daily meditation will help clear your energy of anything that's not in your highest and best interest. Yoga, chanting, and even exercise are other popular ways to clear your energy. In addition, at the start of every day it is best to make sure that you are setting boundaries about what you want to experience.

One way to do this is to imagine yourself surrounded by a

gold circle of light. Set the intention that this circle of light goes with you wherever you go. In this circle of light, only those energies and people that are in your highest and best interest can connect with you. Ask your angels and spirit helpers to amplify the energy of this sacred space. Throughout your day, re-visualize the circle of light around you and ask your angels and helpers to strengthen the energy—this is important if you work around a lot of people or if you're in a high stress or toxic environment.

Also throughout your day I highly recommend asking yourself the question "Where is my energy right now?" And trust your first impression. Does your energy feel scattered or outside of your body? Does it feel like it's stuck around your head and shoulders?

If your energy is not balanced from head to toe within you, then you're unbalanced and more susceptible to other absorbing other people's pain. Unbalanced energy also slows down your ability to manifest and makes it harder for you to understand your intuition. Your pain will be loud and clear when you are unbalanced—in fact, your emotions and thoughts may begin to loop in a 'spiral of doom'. This means that you suddenly start feeling and believing that no matter what you do you'll fail. Your mind starts reminding you of all the times you failed before and all the people who let you down.

If you notice or feel that your energy is unbalanced, say out loud or silently, "Spirit reset my energy and balance it perfectly within me." You can also ground your energy back inside of you by moving your body through dance or exercise, sitting or laying on the ground, sleeping, or taking a hot shower or bath.

Monitoring your energy has to be done constantly throughout the day. Being present with how you feel and what you're observing will help you catch yourself sliding back into the pain vibration. The *Clear Your Energy* exercise in chapter 13 will lead you through a specific process to dissolve the subtle energies that are sabotaging your success.

Moving Forward

The following chapters of this book are focused on specific areas of career success. This book lays a basic foundation of how you can be your own intuitive and manifest a successful career. There is a lot of information in this book and some of it will make more sense to you after you take the actions recommended in each section. Chapter 10 has more details about how to get specific guidance for your unique situation.

CHAPTER 4
ATTRACT CLIENTS & OPPORTUNITIES WITH YOUR GIVE

You can't be successful without other people. Having perfect customers or a great staff or getting mentors and partners that truly support you are examples of how people positively impact your career. What your customers or coworkers experience is more than the actual product or service you provide. You also give them your energy. As discussed in chapter 2, your thoughts, feelings, and emotions are energies that you carry in a magnetic field that surrounds you. What you think and believe attracts people that match the vibration of that energy. Two distinct vibrations that influence the kind of people you attract are Give versus Take. The mindset of Give is connected to your divine brilliance while Take is connected to your pain.

Give vs Take

Focusing on what you provide to others and why that's important to you puts your vibration into the energy of Give. The more that you focus on your Give, the more the universe will give back to you. This doesn't mean that you should work for free or be a people pleaser. Being in the energy of Give means that you believe:

- What you're offering to your customers is high quality
- Your service will truly help your organization/clients in a great way
- You do your best to make sure customer needs are met
- You only have to work with clients who value and respect your service and
- You deserve to be paid the true value of what your services/products are worth

At the opposite end of the spectrum is the Take vibration. A person who's trapped in the energy of Take is constantly thinking about how much is being taken. Either they're worried about taking advantage of other people or they feel like other people are taking advantage of them. This means that they may:

- Often attract difficult people—bosses, coworkers, staff who don't appreciate what they do
- Not respond timely to messages or inquiries from coworkers, customers, and potential clients
- Continually offer discounts for their products and services or keep their prices "low"
- Feel resentful that they do more for others than what they receive in return
- Have difficulty getting enough support from other people to start and/or complete projects
- Attract clients who don't want to pay on time or at all
- Have a hard time getting promoted or closing sales with potential customers

When you are strong in your Give, you know how to price your services and set proper boundaries. Your energy also becomes clear enough to attract more people that want to see you succeed and repel people and situations that drain you.

The Power of Your Give

When you are doing work that you love and sincerely providing your best service to others you create a *healing* space that other people sense and experience. This is true no matter what your industry is or what you do professionally. You hold a space of healing when you sincerely give your best. Other people are attracted to this energy. This doesn't mean that they are a good fit for you. All they know is that when they're around you, they feel better. This may lead to attracting potential customers who take up hours of your time telling you their story only to back out of buying your product. This can also lead to needy people latching onto you, constantly asking for advice or feedback only to ignore what you recommend. They don't really want your advice; they want your healing energy.

This is why it's important to be clear about what you really want to give to others and *how* you want to give it. You also have to be honest about how much energy you're expending to do your best work. Your physical body will tell you how much energy you need for what you have to do. If you find yourself getting tired or exhausted that is a sign you are expending more energy than you're receiving. If you find yourself getting exhausted or extremely irritated after meeting with a specific person or going to a specific place, that is usually a sign that you are giving away your energy and allowing yourself to be drained.

Do you know all that you're giving right now? Here are questions that will help you understand your current Give:

- What services/products are you offering right now? How do you feel when you do those services or provide those products?
- How does what your doing now match your big "why" (as described in chapter 3)?
- List all of the ways that you are currently giving to others right now (include professional and personal life, such as giving advice to friends, paying your kid's tuition, volunteering, etc.) Once your list is done answer these

questions:
- o What on your list really makes you happy, good, inspired, etc.?
- o What on your list makes you feel overwhelmed, annoyed, irritated, or drained?
- o How do the items on your list affect your business/career?
- o What on the list do you wish you could stop doing right now? What do you need now to be able to stop doing those things?
- o What on the list do you wish you could do more of right now? What do you need to be able to do more of those things?

By answering the above questions and getting present with what you are currently experiencing, you will receive intuitive insight from Spirit about what to release from your life or what to do more of. If there is a service you would like to give right now but you aren't sure how to do it, ask Spirit to give you guidance for the best way to implement that idea.

You may have begun to see the ways in which you are operating from a vibration of Take rather than Give. This means that you may be giving your time and energy to people who are draining you or you might be doing things that you really don't want to do.

Continually doing things that you don't want to do blocks your ability to manifest what you desire. The reason is that you're holding your energy hostage in a belief of "I can't really do what I want." You can feel whether or not you truly want to help someone or take an action. If you do something that isn't in your highest and best interest you may feel resentful, annoyed, irritated, guilt, or other discomfort. You may also have had a physical feeling in your body such as your stomach being tied in knots or suddenly feeling tired.

Sometimes it's not possible to stop doing something you don't like. To break through that energy you have to take action doing things that you truly desire.

When I discovered I was intuitive, I had been working for the federal government for 10 years. By that time I knew I didn't want to stay working there but I also knew it wasn't the right time to leave my job. The way I wanted to help people was through using my intuition. I spent my free time developing my own intuition and started my own business, seeing clients and giving workshops. After 5 years of developing my intuition and working with clients, I was able to leave my federal job and be a full-time entrepreneur.

If you are involved in a difficult situation and don't know how to disengage from it, ask Spirit to give you the tools to release yourself from that energy. The meditations in chapters 11 – 13 can help you do this.

Remember that you attract people that match your own vibration. If you feel taken advantage of it is because you aren't valuing and honoring yourself. The rest of this chapter and the sections in chapter 5 will help you better understand your value.

Get Clear With Your Give

Being in the mindset of giving means that you are focused on what you truly want others to experience from the moment they see your logo to how they feel during and after they work with you. When you are clear about what you truly want people to experience, you will get clear about the kind of systems, staff, and support you need to provide the best service. This makes it easy to use your intuition to set prices.

Some people work from the opposite end. Instead of focusing on what they truly want to give, they come up with a price for a product or service first and then try to fit what they do into that price point. This may cause a disconnect in energy where the entrepreneur isn't truly aligned with what they are charging. Potential clients and customers will feel this disconnect and will reflect this back to the business owner. The result is attracting customers who don't want to pay full price for products

41

or who complain that the service is too expensive. This happens even if the business owner is *undercharging* for their services. When you get clear and understand the value of what you are giving, you attract clients who are happy to pay.

When you are clear about how you will support coworkers and staff it makes it easier for your intuition to give you insights about who to hire, what partnerships to form, and how to make powerful connections. If you only focus on what you want people to give you, your energy will pull on their vibration. This happens when you really believe a specific person is necessary for your success. Energetically you are taking their energy and trying to make them responsible for your happiness. That means when you interact with them they'll perceive you as an energy drain. This will cause them to not want to support you or work with you.

To get clear about your Give answer the following questions. Be honest; answer these questions as if you could do anything you wanted instead of answering questions from the standpoint of what you think you can do right now:

- What are the five most important words you would like clients to associate with you and your business?
- What are the five most important words you would like coworkers and/or partners to associate with you and your work?
- What do you truly wish to offer your customers and/or organization right now?
   - What would be the best way for them to get the most out of what you provide?
   - How do you want to give them your service/product?
   - How does this tie back to the five words you want associated with your work?
   - What systems would help you easily give service in the way you desire?
- If applicable, what decorations/furniture do you want in your physical space that match the five words that you

want associated with your business?
- What is it that your clients/organization will receive if they work with you?
    o How will this change their lives?
    o Why is that important right now?
    o How does this tie back to the five words you want them to associate with you?
- What do you want to learn or develop further to help your coworkers and customers?
- What skillsets do you need your staff to have to help you provide the best service possible?

Intuition and Your Give

As you get clear with the experience you would like your customers and coworkers to have, your intuition will give you insights about how to implement what you desire. Your intuition may also give you new and innovative ideas.

One of my clients was a medical esthetician who specialized in youth rejuvenation. She was frustrated that the clients she attracted didn't commit to the regimen she gave them to keep their skin healthy. When she did the above process of getting clear about what she wanted clients to experience, she realized that she wanted women to reclaim their beauty, inside and out, and feel empowered. She knew that she had to help women see that self-care was a necessity. She focused on letting her clients know why it was in their highest and best interest to see her on a recurring basis; she created new packages to make it easy for them to sign up and pay for multiple appointments with her all at once.

As my client created new packages she had a sudden urge (her intuition!) to look at new technology related to skin care. She followed her intuition and was instantly attracted to a special type of equipment. The equipment was expensive, far more than she thought she could afford. She was so drawn to have it that she ignored her worries and bought it. When she did this, she received several impressions and insights (intuition!) about how to implement the new technology and created new services. These packages were very high end. She was worried that no one would want to buy them. I reminded her that her intuition was guiding her to give her best service. She visualized her clients having miracle results very quickly; she connected with Spirit and asked who would benefit the most from her new packages. Specific names dropped into her awareness.

She reached out to those clients; most of them agreed to the new packages. My client was surprised! She was even more surprised when her customers started calling her to say they loved the new service and were seeing miracle results. Soon, her clients invited her to work on their friends—she was able to expand her business from New Mexico to New York.

This example shows how intuition works with the power of your Give. My client didn't get a download to offer this new service until she really tuned into how she wanted to be of service to others. As she received intuitive hits, she took action on them. It was only when she took action that she received more guidance about what to do next. Part of giving her best service meant that she had to restructure what she was currently offering and set boundaries with clients about how they could work with her.

Even though she followed her intuition she still had doubts and worries about what she was doing—the actions she took didn't always make sense to her logical mind, especially when it came to investing money or raising her prices. She believed enough in what she was providing to trust intuition over her fear.

Magnetize Your Give

The moment you decide what you want to offer and whom you want to serve, you will attract people who match that vibration. Something within their energy is resonating with what you're offering. This doesn't guarantee that they'll want to work with you. At the same time you will be attracting people who resonate with your pain, your subconscious limiting beliefs and emotional wounds. It is important to make sure that you market yourself, describe your work, and take actions that are all in alignment with what you want to give and receive. This will make it easy for the people in your highest and best interest to recognize how you can be of service to them. At the same time, you will easily recognize those people who aren't in your highest and best interest and avoid entering into agreements or situations that hinder your career.

Imprint Your Energy

Before you send announcements, create advertisements, or speak to others about your services it is important to make sure you are holding the energy of what you want to provide. Once you strongly feel the energy of your Give, you can actually imprint this energy into your logos, trademarks, advertisements, newsletters, conversations, meetings, and anything else that people come into contact with. When people touch these items or participate in conversations with you, they will feel the energy of your true intentions. To imprint energy:

1. Choose the object that you wish to imprint. If the object is tangible, hold it in your hands (i.e. business cards, invitations, reports, etc.) If the object is intangible such as a business meeting, write the name of what you are imprinting (i.e. workshop, sales call, staff meeting etc.) on a piece of paper and hold the paper in your hand.

2. Look at how you answered the questions in the *Get Clear With Your Give* section of this chapter. Close your eyes and imagine what it would look like, sound like, and feel like to offer this. Imagine how you are impacting your clients' lives in a powerful and uplifting way. Again, use your imagination to focus on what that looks like, feels like, and sounds like to you. If you have a specific message or idea that you would like them to understand focus on what that message is. (Keep it simple.)

3. Imagine how this feels emotionally; experience the gratitude and joy your clients/coworkers will have when they come into contact with you. Add any other emotions you wish them to experience.

4. Imagine the feeling of your emotions and intentions being absorbed into the object or paper you're holding in your hands. Take a few deep breaths and ask Spirit to help you energize this object in the highest and best way. Imagine a white circle of light surrounding the object, holding your intentions with grace.

5. Hand out your object(s) or put your paper in a safe place where it won't be disturbed.

Subtle Energy Traps

Everyone moves back and forth between the energy of Give and Take. The energy is so subtle that most won't even realize they've gone into the Take vibration. The most evident sign that you are not in alignment with your divine brilliance is that you don't have the clients, staff, or support you want. These sections can help you identify where you may be operating out of Take instead of Give.

I'll Take Anything!

Some people, especially those just starting their business or who are new to the workforce are excited to have ANYONE buy a product or hire them. When they think of what qualities they want in a client or a job they just have one: anyone who says yes to me!

If you aren't happy with what's happening in your career, it's time to take a closer look at where you aren't being clear in the type of clients or career you desire. I know there are entrepreneurs who feel like they are open to anyone. I challenge that idea. I'm sure you want clients that are ready, willing, and able to pay you for services as opposed to clients who don't respect what you do and don't want to pay you.

As with everything, the first step in manifesting what you desire is to get specific about the clients and coworkers you want and how you want to be of service to them. If you're unsure what you want it's sometimes helpful to think of what you don't want in a client and look for the opposite qualities. Once you realize what you want it's important to honor your true desires. This means not taking on a client who is not a good fit for you even if you may feel like you really need the money. In fact, it may be time to fire some of your current clients or let go of some of your staff. Your intuition will give you impressions about who is truly in alignment with your career versus who is holding you back.

My Give Is Smaller Than Yours

Part of why staying in the Give vibration is powerful is because it keeps you in sincere alignment with your desire to be of service to others. The universe always supports the energy of that vibration.

Business owners or employees who cut corners and don't do all that they can for their clients and customers will not be in alignment with the vibration of Give. People can sense when someone is holding back and will not want to do business if they think they aren't getting the best value for what they're paying. This can cause businesses to lose customers rapidly. Examples of cutting corners are:

- Not giving your full attention to your client or a project
- Not providing the full level of service you're being paid for
- Doing bare minimum work
- Providing higher levels of service for some more than others who are paying you the same price
- Not being available for coworkers and customers to talk about issues or concerns

Business owners who cut corners usually do so when they experience financial difficulty. Depending on the state of their business, they may feel like they can't afford to provide their clients with the service they wish they could.

If it's on your heart to offer a higher level of service or a greater product, then that is what you should offer. This may mean that you have to charge more for those services. Again, watch where the subtle energy of Take may be come up and convince you that raising your prices would never work. To move through this energy, look at where you feel you may be doing bare minimum or settling for less in your work.

- How is holding back impacting the level of service your customers are receiving?
- What do you need to provide your organization or clients with the best service possible?
- What can you do now to get what you need?

The earlier sections of this chapter will help you use your intuition to get back into the Give vibration and attract the people who can help you experience greater success.

When Others Are In The Take Vibration

You may take all the perfect actions yet potential clients will not want to work with you or you may not be hired or promoted.

It can be frustrating when you think you've made a great connection with a potential client or a hiring official only to have them decide not to work with you. This kind of reaction is normal because of the energy involved.

When a person approaches you they sense on an energetic level that you can truly help them. When you tell them about your services they begin the feel the vibration of support that you will provide and how that support will bring greater miracles into their lives. While they are in that moment with you the energy feels great, it's *exactly* what they need. Then they go home.

When they are away from you the pain and fear of their subconscious mind, sensing that it's about to be changed, goes into full resistance mode. This causes potential clients to have doubts about working with you or buying your products. Deep down they DO truly want your services but their limiting beliefs are blocking them from recognizing that.

You have to believe in what you're offering and not get rattled when people choose not to work with you. The best service you can offer a person who is trapped in the Take vibration is to stay in the power of your Give. Your intuition will guide you on what to say or do. This will vary from person to person. Trust the impressions you receive.

CHAPTER 5
MANIFEST YOUR DESIRED WEALTH

Generating income and making a profit is essential for businesses and career success. What greatly contributes to your ability to earn and keep money is whether or not you feel that you are enough. "I am enough" is a powerful truth of your soul brilliance and is linked to "I deserve" and "I have." Sadly, many people have the limiting belief that they aren't enough. The pain of "I am not enough" ripples through their lives affecting more than just their finances.

At any time a person has the ability to strengthen their conscious connection to their soul truth. This means they can strengthen the "*I am enough*" vibration and let go of not being enough. To better understand how to shift this energy, it's important to understand the vibration of money itself.

The Energy of Money

By itself money has no real value. Paper money is just paper. Gold, silver, diamonds, and other jewels are just rocks. Human beings agreed on a system assigning values to the rocks and the paper. Money is the common language we use to understand the perception of what we're providing and receiving.

Money, like everything else you encounter in life, is a mirror-vibration, it reflects back to you your own beliefs about what you're worth and what you're allowed to receive. This is why to earn more money the focus has to be on how you value yourself and how you perceive the value of what you offer.

The Mirror Vibration In Action

Years ago I was teaching a workshop about the energy of money. I met a client who had spent months applying for jobs but wasn't being hired. He told me that he'd been doing affirmations and meditations with no luck and had come to the workshop to learn how to connect to abundance. Spirit told me, "He *is* connected."

In my intuitive awareness, Spirit showed me an image of Pink Floyd's *Dark Side of The Moon* album cover. On that album is a triangle shaped prism. A ray of white light connects with one side of the prism and a rainbow of multicolored light flows out the other side. The image changed and I saw that there were distortions in the prism—instead of a rainbow of light flowing out of the other side, only bits and pieces of light were seeping out.

Spirit was giving me a visual of how we manifest financial abundance. We are always connected to the energy of prosperity, the ray of white light, and we are always manifesting that prosperity. Our energy, which is made up of our soul, emotions, thoughts, and beliefs, is the prism. As we connect with the energy of financial abundance, our pain, the energy of our limiting beliefs, distorts the energy as it flows through us—instead of flowing out like a rainbow we get bits and pieces of what we truly want.

This was great news! I told my client that he was already manifesting abundance—he was manifesting exactly what his energy wanted based on his subconscious beliefs and feelings. My client was skeptical. He was 100% sure he didn't want to be jobless and broke.

"What do you think about people who have a lot of money?" I asked. He thought for a moment and told me he had come from a wealthy family. In his opinion, many of his rich family members were greedy, self-centered, and self-righteous. As he spoke he realized that he had assigned an emotional value to money—that if *he* had money he would be just like his family, self-centered and greedy. This was why he was unable to get a job—he didn't want to be like his family. His money situation was reflecting back his hidden belief.

He went on to say that he hadn't worked for years and other people had been supporting him throughout his life. Ironically, many of his friends and family members were accusing him of being selfish and self-centered because he was relying on other people to take care of him. From his pain, he had manifested the very situation he was afraid of experiencing.

As I saw more clients who had trouble generating income, I saw a pattern where the very thing they feared around having money was the very thing that they were already manifesting, even if they were broke!

What would be the worst thing about having all the money you desired? What do you resent about others who have money? Where are you experiencing that same fear and resentment in your life right now? Use the meditations in chapters 11 – 13 to release these fears and worries.

How You Spend Is How They Spend

When I first started my business, I went to many classes and workshops. One of the teachers I saw was a professional healer who was teaching how to make money doing spiritual work. He'd been in business for 20 years. He told our class that dealing with cash was best because you could avoid counting it as taxable income. When he said that my energy tanked, I suddenly felt tired and sick to my stomach.

I had absorbed his victim energy, the energy of lack. The

feeling was amplified by some of the students in the room who had the same feelings—many were used to struggling financially. I found out later that even though he'd been in business for 20 years, he'd spent most of those years barely making ends meet.

Money is a mirror vibration. The way you view *spending* money will be the way that people view paying you for your services. If you feel like you shouldn't have to pay much for things or if you always want to buy goods and services as cheap as possible, you will attract clients who will act that way when it comes to your services. If you are acting without integrity by not paying taxes you will attract people who aren't in integrity when paying you. If you are having issues with generating income, really look at how you spend:

- Do you resent having to pay for things?
- Do you pay all of your bills on time or are you late, even if you have the money?
- Do you always try to get the cheapest price possible?
- Do you find yourself complaining about what you have buy?

If you don't like spending money you don't have to go on a shopping spree but you do have to change your attitude. You can do this by looking closer at why you don't like to spend money and what you would like instead.

- What do you want people to feel when they pay for your services?
- Is that how you feel when you pay for things?
- What adjustments will you make in your attitude when you buy things from now on?

Taking the simple step of saying that you are thankful for paying a bill will help you shift your perception of paying. There might be times where you have to fake it to make it. You can ask Spirit to give you the understanding of what it's like to be happy to spend.

Also look at non-financial debts you may have with others.

What have you promised to give to someone or do for someone that you haven't done yet? Do you keep your word? Not just with clients but with friends and family members as well? Now is the time to make good on what you promised. The more that you pay your debts, including making good on your promises to people, the more you will experience more people paying you what they owe.

If you don't have an issue with spending money but you still have issues generating consistent income, it's time to take a deeper look at whether or not you truly see yourself as valuable.

Nurture "I Am Enough"

The five steps to manifest success (chapter 3) will help you generate financial prosperity, specifically connecting with Spirit and getting guidance for what actions to take next. When you get intuitive guidance, your pain, the combination of your emotional wounds and subconscious limiting beliefs may convince you not to listen. The limiting belief of "*I am not enough*" is the louder voice in your head, telling you "you can't do that; that'll never work" or "you should just be happy with what you have."

Your pain can also exhaust you by triggering your body to go into stress or by ramping up your emotions, making you too terrified and overwhelmed to take a step. Once you identify the pain for what it is, a limiting belief that is probably not even yours, the energy of "*I am not enough*" will lessen and you will hear your intuition more clearly. You may still feel some overwhelm and anxiety but you can move through it.

You don't have to wait until you've cleared every limiting belief within your system to generate wealth. It's only necessary to know the difference between operating from your divine brilliance versus when you're operating from your pain.

Use your power of discernment to start recognizing and separating the energy of pain from the energy of your brilliance. When you have a strong feeling about something or someone or if you are concerned about whether or not you are making the right decision, stop and ask yourself "is this coming from my pain or my brilliance?"

Trust your first impression when you ask the question. You may feel the answer in your body or get a knowing or images or thoughts in your mind.

If you're feeling stressed, scared, overwhelmed, angry, or any other seemingly negative emotion regarding money, surrender that emotion to Spirit. To do this, say, "I surrender [name the negative emotion or thought you're feeling]." For example, "I surrender being broke" or "I surrender feeling like I'm not enough."

Surrendering your struggle with money gives you the permission to experience your emotions without judging yourself for having them. The more that you practice surrender, the more that pain will be released from your vibration. If you are struggling with a very deep emotional wound, it may take a long period of consistent surrender (such as surrendering the same emotion once a day for 30 days) before you start noticing a difference. Chapter 13 will help you surrender the energy of your limiting beliefs.

Stand In Your Power

Do you allow clients to pay you late (or not at all) or do you bend over backwards to help people who don't appreciate what you do? If so you are experiencing a subtle form of people pleasing, a limiting belief that is allowing people to walk all over you.

Underneath the sweet, kind exterior of a people-pleaser is someone who carries deep resentment, confusion, and anger. People-pleasers want to be liked and continually look for approval from others. The reason is that without someone telling them that they're liked, they don't know if they're really good enough.

Money is a reflection of perceived value. A person with a

strong people-please vibration doesn't know if they're valuable—they rely on other people to make that decision for them. They then feel taken advantage of when their clients and coworkers don't value them.

This doesn't mean you shouldn't give something extra to your peers or customers. It does mean that you have to be present with *why* they're doing something extra. This goes back to the question asked above: are you operating from pain or your brilliance? Are you only offering that extra service because you want this person's approval or because it's on your heart to do so?

If you find yourself constantly doing favors for clients, friends, and family and you get annoyed or resentful when you're actually giving them the favor, then that is a sign from your intuition that it's not in your highest and best interest to do those extra things. If you really do feel happy and appreciative when you give more than you receive, that is your intuition saying "yes!"

Don't assume that your clients and coworkers know how to treat you. Only you know how you want to be treated. This is where being clear and setting strong boundaries up front with people will help set the tone of what you both can expect. Answering the questions below will help you shift through people-please energy and stand in your power:

- Which of your clients, coworkers, or partners are draining your energy? What have you said to them about the situation? What boundary will you put in place to stop the energy drain?
- Where do you need stronger rules in place? (Such as rules about being on time, after-hour phone calls, client preparedness?) How will you communicate these rules to your clients and partners?
- Where else in your life do you feel like others are taking advantage of you? What are you willing to change?

If you don't respect yourself enough to set clear boundaries with others, you are reinforcing the energy that you aren't good enough to be respected. This affects your financial situation. The more that you stand in your power, the more you will attract other people who will recognize the value of what you're providing.

Price Your Services Correctly

How *you* see the value of your services is what will be reflected back to you in how much money you earn. When you aren't charging your true value you will be affected energetically by the gap you are creating. The gap is the difference between the amount of energy you are giving and the amount of money you are receiving for your products/services. Here are five signs that you are undercharging for your services (especially if two or more apply to your situation):

1. You get extremely exhausted after and/or in between meeting with clients
2. You feel overwhelmed by the high volume of clients you have to see
3. You start complaining that you should be charging more for your services/you feel resentful or irritated that clients don't appreciate the value of what you're providing
4. Clients suddenly stop coming to you
5. You get sick more often than usual on the days when you have clients scheduled

If you work for someone else and have two or more signs of undercharging for services, it may be time to ask for a raise or look for promotion opportunities.

If you're a business owner, you may be resistant to the idea of raising your prices even if you recognize that you are undercharging. This is where the pain of your limiting beliefs will say, "people can't afford to pay me more than that!" or "I can't charge more than what other people are charging, I'll lose business to competition."

Most of my clients who raised the prices of their services saw an increase in business almost immediately afterward. This is because their energy was finally in alignment with what they were charging. The value of what they were receiving matched the value of what they were giving. This is manifesting from brilliance versus manifesting from pain.

If you are getting the intuitive nudge that it's time to raise your prices, do it. Remember your intuition is always 100% correct. The longer that you continue to undercharge for your services you will begin to affect your health—this isn't a woo-woo concept. If you expend more time and energy than what you are receiving you will exhaust your physical body. Another side effect of undercharging is that the energy of your discomfort will be so strong that you repel clients from working with you.

How many times have you given your services for free or for discounted prices only to be met with a person who argues with you, resists what you're offering, or minimizes what you do? This happens because you are undervaluing yourself and the people around you are mirroring that energy back to you.

Asking people to pay you what your services are worth does not harm them. If you struggle with feeling as though you're taking from someone read chapter 4. By charging the true value of your services, you're holding the energy of "I am good enough" and "I deserve this."

Understand Your Value

Clients and customers are not just paying for your time or your product. They're paying for your experience, your expertise, and ability to help them. All the lessons that you have learned, all the education and training you've received, all the healing and inner work that you've done, and all the time and money you have invested into your development is part of the value that you provide. You gain more experience and expertise with every client you see which means that the value of what you provide is constantly increasing.

Some entrepreneurs fear that if they charge more than someone else, clients will flock to the cheaper competition. As long as you are truly aligned with what you're offering and what the value of that service is, this will not be an issue. Most people expect to get more value if they spend more. It's up to you to keep focusing on your Give (see chapter 4) so that potential customers understand the value of what you're providing.

Some of my clients who raised their prices found that resistance about their price increase came from other entrepreneurs in their industry NOT their customers. People who complain about someone else's prices are projecting how they value themselves onto others. Those people who are the most blocked, who see the least value in themselves will protest the loudest. Their complaining has nothing to do with you or your services.

By standing in your own power and honoring your value you will empower other people to do the same.

Set Prices With Intuition

I don't believe in basing prices solely off of what someone else is doing. You can use an industry standard as a starting point but then use your intuition to tune into where your rates should be. Below is an exercise that will help you use your intuition to feel the value of what you're providing and know what you should be paid. This exercise can also be used to help you set salaries for your staff. To get the most out of this process be sure that you are clear about what you are providing to others and how that feels to you as discussed in chapter 4.

To use your intuition to set correct prices:

1. Take deep breaths. With every breath in, imagine that white light is flowing into your heart and spreading throughout the inside of your entire body. With every breath out, imagine you are releasing fear, doubt, and confusion.

2. When you feel centered and relaxed, ask Spirit to join you.

3. Think about the service or product you are offering (if you offer multiple services, focus on just one right now.) Sit with the feeling of what it's like to offer that service.

4. Think of the current price you are charging for that service. As you sit with that current price pay attention to how you feel in your physical body. Do you notice any tension? Heaviness? Tiredness? Anxiety? Discomfort? Those are signs the price is too low.

5. Add $100 (or more/less) to that price. Focus on how that feels. Did anything shift? Does that new number feel more comfortable or the same? Does the price need to go higher or lower? Trust your first impression, not the voice in your head that says "no one will pay me that!"

6. Keep adding $100 (or more/less) to the price until it feels right in your body. This means you will feel energized, calm, peaceful, or any discomfort you felt before will vanish. If your price is too low or too high you will feel discomfort in your body.

7. When you feel that you have the right price, repeat this exercise for any other services you're providing.

Focus On Prosperity

It can be easy to get frustrated if you are having difficulty with finances. At times, it may even seem impossible to change your circumstances. Everyone goes through phases of doubt, fear, and frustration. The key is not to get stuck in the negativity. Remember, you are always manifesting what you believe. The more that you say to yourself "things will never change" or "I'll always be broke" the more that you will continue to manifest things not changing and being broke.

This doesn't mean that you have to fake happiness. You

have to honor your emotions and acknowledge them as they happen, even if they're negative. There is a clear difference between acknowledging negative feelings and wallowing in your same old story. Every time you think and feel from your pain instead of your brilliance, you are delaying your success.

The way to accelerate earning more money is to focus on the feeling that you would like to experience if you had more wealth. The more that you go into the energy of what you would like your financial experience to be, the easier it will be to attract the opportunities that will manifest that reality.

As you release your limiting beliefs around not being enough, you may suddenly experience more financial challenges that seem to spring up out of nowhere. This is a sign that you're letting go of pain from deeper levels of your subconscious. Your energy shifts and clears in cycles. This means you will have a profound breakthrough and then see an old issue rise up again but with far less intensity. It is also common to experience something that really upsets you and makes you want to give up right before you experience a life-changing miracle.

Don't allow your mind to convince you that you're stuck or that you haven't changed. Surrender any of those feelings to Spirit using the techniques in this chapter.

Subtle Energy Traps

The pain vibration of *"I am not enough"* affects your financial situation in a variety of ways. Below are two of the most common issues I see when working with clients and techniques to overcome them.

Addicted To Broke

Pain can be a very comfortable feeling. Some people don't realize the full extent of what they're truly feeling. To a person in this situation, they will see that they aren't having the financial success they want but they don't see any solutions. *"That's just how it is"* is a common saying for people in this vibration. When they hear career or business advice, they don't think advice applies to their situation and will come up with continual excuses for why they can't do something.

If you are hesitant to make changes in your career yet you continually feel stressed out about your current situation you may be addicted to the pain of feeling as though you aren't enough. If you really believed that you could have what you wanted, you would take action. Something in your energy has convinced you that no matter what you do, your situation will stay the same. So why try at all? Perfectionism and procrastination are more subtle forms of this energy. More information for dealing with those vibrations can be found in chapter 6, *Accelerate Your Success.*

If you are having issues with money, hooray! If you *see* your pain you can shift through it. The very act of connecting with Spirit and focusing on what you truly desire will reset your energy. Focusing on the five steps of manifesting (chapter 3), especially steps 1 – 3 will help you the most with believing in yourself and feeling your true power. This will also help you get the courage and inspiration you need to make changes in your situation.

Doing Me A Favor

People affected by the subtle energy of *"I am not enough"* often have great difficulty when they are presented with a genuine business or career opportunity that will bring in more income. Instead of standing in their power, they will retreat back into their pain. This means that they let other people walk over them or they'll agree to deals that aren't in their highest and best interest. The energy they are putting out to the world says, "You're doing me a favor."

The energy of "you're doing me a favor" reinforces the subconscious limiting belief that the entrepreneur hasn't really done enough to deserve the opportunity. They may take on their first "big" client but not hold that client to the same standards as other customers or they may agree to a lesser salary when accepting a job opportunity. Later on, when the initial excitement of the opportunity wears off, the person may feel resentful about what they agreed to do.

One of my clients was a gifted fashion designer who had a full time day job working in a corporate office. He wanted to leave his day job but he needed more buyers who were interested in his pieces. When it came to selling his designs, he visited local boutiques to see if they would be willing to carry his pieces. Boutique owners were interested in meeting with him to talk about more about his designs.

When it came close to the day of the meeting, my client could feel himself getting scared. He told me that when he met with the boutique owners he was going to ask for the lowest possible price, just to cover his costs. He didn't want the boutique owners to think that he was trying to take advantage of them.

This energy was forming a subtle trap. If he went in with a very low price he was going to send a mixed message by undervaluing his products.

Selling your services for an extremely low price or accepting a low salary doesn't show another person that you're being grateful. Most people have no frame of reference for how valuable your product or service is—they rely on *you* to make that determination. If you give them a cheap price all they'll know is that your value is cheap.

If my client offered the boutique owner a low price he would be setting himself up for the expectation that his brand was low-end. For some business owners having a low-dollar product is perfectly in alignment with their business values. For my client, it wasn't.

My client came up with a set price for his pieces and offered discounts to stores if they bought in bulk. This resonated with the boutiques; he was able to get his designs into stores without having to give his work away. By standing in his power he formed a partnership with the boutiques rather than setting up a toxic relationship where he would later be resentful about the boutiques not respecting his worth.

If you are presented with a business opportunity, tune into the energy of that opportunity before saying yes or no. To do this, think of your divine vision and your true business goals. When you are really feeling the energy, think of the opportunity your being presented with and notice what you feel in your physical body. Does the opportunity make you feel uncomfortable, tired, or uneasy? If so, this is a "no" or a sign that terms would have to be changed in order for you to accept. If you feel good, confident, energized, strong, or clear, those are signs that it is okay to say "yes."

Trust your first impression and stand in your power when new opportunities are presented to you. In most cases, no one is doing you a favor. You *earned* your opportunities.

CHAPTER 6
ACCELERATE YOUR SUCCESS

Intuition has the potential to increase your success in a short period of time. However, intuition alone won't produce results. The energy of your divine vision has to be anchored in reality before it can manifest. This comes down to action versus inaction. Your brilliance never has any reason to hesitate. It's fearless. The pain of your subconscious limiting beliefs tells you to slow down and feeds you worries and doubts about moving forward.

It's not necessary to keep manifesting from the slow lane. The more that you stay mindful of what you want and how you are feeling the easier it is to understand your intuition and take actions from your divine brilliance. When you do that, you generate income, complete projects, and get dream jobs faster than you ever have before. If you get caught up in the drama of "this is taking too long" you slip into the energy of your pain and manifest more blocks to getting what you want.

The Missing Link
I know people who have prayed for years on one specific

issue and do several affirmations a day for that issue yet their situation doesn't seem to improve. This is because there's a disconnect between the energy of their divine vision and the energy of reality. The missing link is consistent action. Taking repeated action is what grounds the energy of your intention into the world.

Imagine that you and Spirit are sitting side by side in a rowboat in the middle of a lake. When you and Spirit row the boat together, the boat will move fast across the water. However, if you refuse to pick up the oar, Spirit will continue to paddle but the boat may not go in the direction you want. There's not enough energy to move you forward.

When a person consciously connects with Spirit they get an extra push of energy to manifest their desires in a faster way. If they take immediate and consistent actions that are in alignment with their divine vision, they create a vortex of energy where miracles and opportunities are pulled toward them.

Consistent actions have to be taken whether your career is doing great or not so great. An entrepreneur who stops doing as much marketing or networking when their business is doing well will experience the results of that slow down, though it may not happen right away.

In chapter 3 in the *Ask Spirit For Guidance* section I showed you how you could get specific action steps from Spirit using your intuition. Following those actions will help you go to the next level of success in your business. The longer that you wait to take action on what you were told, you risk diminishing the result you could have gotten had you taken action right away.

If you feel stuck in your business, like nothing is moving forward, it is important to take an action that you can complete 100%. This action has to be something that is important to you but it doesn't have to be related to your business. For example, if you've been meaning to clean your kitchen or mow your lawn and that really matters to you, do it. The energy of completing an action that is on your heart to do will move the energy of you and your business into a stronger flow.

Keeping your energy clear also helps. Meditation is a great way to do this. There are many different types of meditation, including walking meditations and chanting. Yoga and dancing are physical ways to connect and clear your energy. Find the form that works best for you. At times it is also necessary to get help from another person such as visiting a hypnotherapist or energy healer to help you clear intense resistance.

The Unsexy Vibration of Change

A client of mine was feeling stuck. She wanted me to tune in and tell her what else to do to generate income right away. When I tuned in with my intuition, I clearly felt and saw that my client knew exactly what to do to generate that income. She didn't agree. "I've done everything I can do and the money's not here," she said.

"What haven't you done that you know you need to do?" I asked. The client admitted that they hadn't called back all of the people they'd met at a conference and they hadn't finished sending out invoices to clients who had signed up for services. My client hadn't done those things because she assumed they weren't going to make a real difference. She was making assumptions and taking action (or not taking action) from the energy of her pain instead of the energy of her brilliance.

Her subconscious limiting beliefs had convinced her that she had done *everything* and that the only way out of her situation was to get a miracle from somewhere else. The more that we spoke my client realized that she had actually been given multiple opportunities to generate income. Instead of staying present with what she was doing and completing actions, her mind had talked her into giving up.

When entrepreneurs have a new business goal or a person gets a new job it can be very exciting. At first they feel motivated to do whatever it takes to reach their goals. After a while, the excitement can be replaced with a feeling of tediousness. This is the unsexy phase of change, when a person is working hard, taking all the right actions but feels discouraged because they don't think they're getting results.

Their limiting beliefs can convince them that there's no way to change their situation. This is the point where people give up on an idea or their entire business altogether, not realizing they were about to manifest significant success.

I have consistently seen that the closer my clients are to achieving a big business goal, the more their subconscious limiting beliefs come up. This is because they are finally breaking through the limiting energy and their subconscious mind is struggling to keep the old pain in tact. If my clients start believing what their subconscious mind is telling them, they move into the vibration of manifesting from their pain. This slows down their ability to get results.

To make it through this phase, it is crucial to have a good support team to help you stay motivated and hold you accountable for taking consistent actions toward your goal. This may mean having to hire coaches or meet with mentors or even join a mastermind group.

It is also important to make sure that the actions you take are truly in alignment with your divine vision and that you aren't doing anything that feels like a burden or energy drain. This may mean hiring support staff or investing in a new system to do certain tasks you don't like to do or letting go of clients you can't stand.

Depending on your financial situation the idea of hiring someone else or letting go of a paying client may seem scary. It doesn't have to be. Remember, potential clients feel your energy; if you are constantly stressed and overwhelmed they will be repelled by what they feel in your vibration. When you let go of what's draining you and get support you have more energy to focus on your business. Your intuition will let you know when you need to get more help or let go of something that's not serving you. Your intuition will keep repeating the same guidance over and over until you take action.

Energy Accelerators

When you take consistent actions in alignment with your divine truth, you accelerate seeing results. Here are some of the most common ways to work with the energy around you to expedite your success:

1. **Put yourself in the energy that you want to experience.**

   Like attracts like. The more that you feel the energy of what you're moving toward, the more that you put yourself in a magnetic vibration where you attract miracles and opportunities. This means joining organizations or spending time with people who have achieved your goal. It can also mean putting yourself in physical locations or giving yourself specific experiences that mirror the energy of your desires.

   • If you dream of being a multimillionaire entertainer, go to concerts or events where there are multimillionaire entertainers performing. Spend time with entertainers who are taking actions to manifest their goals. Spend time visiting high-end shops. Buy clothes and accessories that make you feel like a multimillionaire entertainer.

   • If you dream of being a world speaker, go see other world speakers, read their books, join organizations that are geared toward helping people speak from a world stage.

   • If you dream of being a famous chef, go to Michelin-star restaurants, watch interviews with your favorite celebrity chefs. Find other chefs who are interested in doing the same thing and are taking successful actions. Buy a special chef jacket with your name on it or kitchen tools that make you feel like an accomplished chef.

2. **Get rid of clutter from your home, car, and workspace.**

   The energy of the past can reside in objects, especially where there's clutter. This doesn't necessarily mean that the energy is 'bad' it just may not be in alignment with who you are now. Cluttered spaces can trap energy and lead to making you feel tired, overwhelmed, and stuck. Throw out old clothes or items that don't resonate with you anymore, replace old and worn items you don't like. Hire help if you need it. Cleaning your space is important.

3. **Experience gratitude and appreciation.**

   Consciously think of what you're thankful for throughout your day. Thank yourself and thank Spirit for showing up. The more you connect with these vibrations, the easier it is for you manifest from your brilliance.

4. **Reward Yourself First.**

   Some clients actually hold off on taking vacations or even getting their hair done until they feel like they've 'earned' it. This is holding your happiness hostage and only reinforces the energy that you can't have what you want unless you work hard. Doing what makes you happy invites greater joy, gratitude, and thankfulness into your life, which will help you have more energy to manifest what you desire. Watch a movie; go dancing—whatever it is that makes you happy, do it.

5. **Get Support.**

   You may quickly realize that you can't do everything alone if you want to give the best service. The right support staff can free your energy so you can focus on your true work. Getting support may also mean hiring a business coach or mentor or joining a group that can help you stay focused on your goals and give you the right knowledge and motivation to keep taking action.

Energy Drains

Just like certain actions can speed up your progress, you can unknowingly make it harder to manifest your goals by how you behave and what you think. The following actions slow down your ability to manifest:

1. **Keeping yourself in the same old energy.**

   Really be mindful of who's around you and where you're spending your time. If you continually put yourself with people or in situations that are not anywhere close to what you want to experience, you will slow the energy of manifesting your desires. Some people feel obligated to spend time with family members or friends that they know are energy drains. This has a ripple effect that can negatively impact how you show up in your work. This doesn't mean you have to drop your friends but it does mean you should make the effort to spend time in the energy you want to be part of and minimize your time around people who aren't in alignment with where you're going. Remember like attracts like.

2. **Blaming others for your situation.**

   The energy of your limiting beliefs can be so subtle that you don't even realize that you're the one sabotaging your own success. On the surface it looks like other people or institutions or systems are to blame for your experience. The more present that you are, meaning, the more that you are aware of what you're truly feeling, thinking, and experiencing, you will start to see where others are reflecting your own limiting beliefs back to you. This is empowering because once you see your limiting beliefs you can take steps to change them and accept responsibility for your happiness.

3. **Blaming yourself for your situation.**

   Taking responsibility for your happiness is not the same as blaming yourself. The energy of blame is toxic. If you are putting yourself down or living with regret about your actions, you are draining your own energy and making it harder to manifest what you would like. Self-blame is a form of victim energy. It goes hand-in-hand with low self-esteem. Forgive yourself for anything you regret doing or not-doing in the past. Give yourself the permission to have a different experience now. Be very mindful of what you're thinking and saying to yourself. The more that you criticize yourself the more you are locking yourself in the energy of pain.

4. **Giving Up.**

   If you don't complete projects or don't take consistent action you won't generate enough energy to create what you would like. Sometimes an entrepreneur is taking actions but they are just going through the motions, they've mentally checked out. This form of giving up can also slow down progress because you stop connecting with the power of Spirit. This can lead to self-sabotage.

5. **Being Unclear.**

   Every action you take has to be in alignment with your divine vision. If you stray from what you really want to do, you send a mixed message to the universe and get mixed results. Being clear means honoring how you feel; if you are afraid or in pain and you force yourself to be positive, you stop being clear about what you're experiencing. Being unclear makes it harder for you to understand your intuition. When you sense pain in yourself, be present and surrender it, don't ignore it.

If you struggle with any of these energy slow-downs read chapter 13 for a special breathing exercise to clear your energy.

Remember to Rest

There are times when you have to take a break. Your intuition will let you know when you need to stop and rest. This usually happens when you wake up and suddenly have the urge to stay in bed or go to the movies. You may even catch yourself saying, "I need a vacation" or "I just need a minute to myself." Pay attention to what you are saying you need and how your body feels. If you are physically or mentally exhausted, you will not be able to get strong intuitive guidance. Working while burned out will only lead to you manifesting from your pain. When you rest, your subconscious limiting beliefs may kick in and try to make you feel guilty for taking a break. Ignore those thoughts and honor yourself.

If you're ever unsure when you should take an action or whether to rest you can ask yourself the question "Should I do this now?" and trust your first impression. If the answer is "no," trust it.

Subtle Energy Traps

There are many reasons why people don't take consistent action. Most of these reasons come from the pain of their subconscious yet on the surface it may 'make sense' to the person who is procrastinating. Below are some of the subtle energies that slow down the manifestation process and how to overcome those challenges:

Waiting For Perfect

When I worked for the federal government I used to hear the motto *done is better than perfect.* If our organization waited to implement systems until everything was perfect, we'd never complete anything. This didn't mean we did a half-ass job; we genuinely did our best to put systems and procedures into place that had a strong foundation. At the same time we understood that we probably had missed an issue that we'd have to correct later.

Perfection is a subtle energy vibration that is closely connected to fear of moving outside of the comfort zone of pain. Perfectionism can cause a person to be caught in active non-action. From their perspective, it looks like they're getting things in order so everything will be 'perfect' but in reality they're just stalling.

I remember when I decided that it was time to do intuitive readings professionally. I told myself that in order to have a business, I would need business cards. I wanted a business card with my picture on it, which meant I needed professional headshots. In order to get headshots I had to get my hair done. Because I was African-American and living in Albuquerque New Mexico I couldn't find a black hair salon I liked. "So," I told myself, "I guess I can't start a business right now" and I did nothing for six months. I really believed that if God wanted me to be in business, he'd send a black hairdresser to Albuquerque! In my mind I had done all that I could do. I couldn't start my business until everything was *perfect.*

I share this story because many of your subconscious limiting beliefs may be hiding behind the blind spot of perfection. This blind spot can be so massive that you may not even see how ridiculous and irrational your thought process is.

Where are you holding yourself back because you want to be perfect? What do you really need to reach your goal versus what you're telling yourself that you need?

Use your intuition and ask Spirit, "what projects do I need to complete right now?" and "what action do I take next?" Trust your first impression and follow your guidance.

Waiting For Permission
The subtle energy of wanting permission is strongly tied to

people pleasing. A client of mine came to one of our sessions very upset, he had shared a new business plan with his spouse; his spouse thought the idea was stupid. My client was now angry that his spouse wasn't supportive. He also wasn't sure if his business plan really was stupid.

He had taken what his spouse said to heart. By doing that, he gave his power away. Giving his power away meant that he didn't have to take responsibility for his actions. If he wasn't responsible for his actions, nothing was ever his fault. In this situation he was blaming his spouse for sabotaging his career. In reality he was sabotaging his own career by waiting for someone to give him permission to do what he wanted.

There are times when it's important to ask someone for assistance or advice. People who have a problem with waiting for permission before taking action don't ask advice from people who can truly help them, they ask for advice from people they want approval from. They want someone else to validate their feelings because they don't trust themselves. If you feel you need someone else's guidance, advice, or opinion consider these questions about the person you're going to ask:

- Does this person truly have knowledge or a skillset in the area of expertise I need guidance in?
- Am I inspired by what this person does in the area of expertise I need guidance in?
- Does this person normally give well-rounded advice or do they come from a perspective of fear and limitation?
- Is the person going to give me advice for what I should do in my situation or will they give advice from what *they* would do in my situation?
- Do I really need advice from this person or am I only asking because I'm afraid to trust the decision I already made?

By answering the questions above you may realize that you can ask for advice from someone in one specific area but not in another. When it comes to your career be mindful of when you truly need assistance versus when you're just looking for permission to do what you know you want to do.

Avoiding Failure

Similar to the subtle energy of perfection, the fear of making a mistake can sometimes be so crippling that people never take action. Or they may start a project and then give up if it doesn't seem to be coming together easily. Ironically, this can happen in the area of the business that the entrepreneur cares the most about. People who are affected by this energy won't be able to stay motivated or focused, even though they are doing what they love.

The subconscious mind is trying to protect the person from failing their "big" dream. If they never take action, they'll never fail. Their dreams remain perfectly in tact. Ironically, this leads to the person never having their dream life because they didn't pursue it.

If you have goals that you deeply desire completing but can't seem to get it done, really decide if you are committed to making that goal a reality. Then get professional help. Whether that's a business mentor, writing coach, art program, or some other type of expert, having someone in your life who's only mission is to see you succeed will help you push through the fear of failure. Coaches and mentors can also keep you motivated and hold you accountable to take action.

I Already Know That! (But my career still sucks)

It's easy to get caught up in the routine of day-to-day life to the point where we think we've seen it all, done it all, and know it all when it comes to our career. This can lead to becoming complacent instead of innovative and cause stagnation in a business.

An extremely negative aspect of the "I already know that" vibration causes people to not take consistent action. When they take actions and don't see instantaneous results, they move on to something else without building enough energy for success to manifest. Some will stop taking actions altogether because they feel so stuck.

A colleague of mine was frustrated that she didn't get promoted into a new position that had been created in her department. She was convinced that person who got the job had been pre-selected by the supervisors even though many people had applied for the job. I suggested that she go to her supervisors and get feedback on her application. She hesitated then admitted that she hadn't even applied for the job. "But that was because it was so rigged! I just knew it!" She said. Her "I already know that" energy cost her an opportunity to be considered for the job. In her mind she was completely justified in not taking the action. Her mind also reassured her that not getting the job was someone else's fault!

Consistently following the five steps to manifesting success listed in chapter 2 will help you break through the "I already know that" barrier to manifest what you desire.

For a person stuck in this vibration it is very important to take action steps and focus on keeping their attitude positive without feeling like a victim or blaming other people, situations, or institutions for their challenges.

CHAPTER 7
GET SUPPORT IN ALL THE RIGHT PLACES

The reason why intuition is so effective in helping you manifest career success is because you are partnering with Spirit. In addition to partnering with Spirit, it is important to have support from other people. The right support can make the difference between having a mediocre career to becoming a powerful center of influence.

When a person first starts their business they may have to do almost everything in that business: answer phones, do the accounting, clean the office, create a website, plan events, etc, in addition to the actual business work that they do. As time goes on they will find that it is very hard to keep doing *everything* and still provide the level of service that they want to give to their customers. This impacts their income.

For salaried employees, they may be used to shining on their own but will find that in order to get promoted or make a bigger impact in their organization they need support from their coworkers.

If you want to go to the next level of success in your industry you can't do it alone. This means you may have to hire staff, invest in technology and systems, and/or getting special support specifically for you to help take your skills and success to the next level.

Some people cringe at the thought of having to involve someone else in their career. They may have had experiences where other people let them down.

Many of the people that hire me as their coach feel alone on their journey, even if they are married or have families. They are receiving a strong call to action from their soul. he people in their lives may not understand how it feels to have a strong soul calling—this is especially true if those people are disconnected from their own soul truth.

A coach or a mentor only has one job: help you get phenomenal results. The focus is all about you and how to succeed. The simple act of having one person who believes in you and also wants your success amplifies your ability to achieve that success. This is why hiring a coach or finding a mentor can be a powerful experience.

Entrepreneur groups and masterminds are also great. When many people come together for a similar purpose, it amplifies the energy of everyone's intention in a greater way.

Your intuition works well with concepts and ideas that you understand. If you don't understand how to do something then your intuition can only give you general insights about that issue. When you hire an expert in that area your intuition can give you more specific guidance as you learn more about the process. For example, if you don't know how to do taxes, your intuition may guide you to hiring a tax professional. As you work with that professional, you will receive more specific impressions about what to ask them to do, how to involve them in other aspects of your business, and more.

Don't Delay

You know when you need help. You will start feeling overwhelmed and/or frustrated with your current situation. You may also have issues with scheduling clients, delivering products, or completing tasks in a timely manner.

Even though a person needs support, many people wait until they are in a tremendous amount of pain, either financially or personally, before they decide to get the help they need. This isn't necessary. Your intuition will let you know right away when you need support. The longer that you wait, the worse off you may get. Remember, Spirit will keep repeating the same ideas to you over and over. If you find yourself saying, "it'd be nice if someone could help me with this" pay attention. That's your intuition speaking to you.

If you're truly unsure when or how to get support, ask Spirit! Trust the first impression you receive. Many of my clients are surprised that when they finally get clear about the support they need, the person that can help them the most seems to magically show up in their lives. It isn't magic, it's you manifesting what's in your highest and best interest. Take action before you get into crisis.

Get The Support You Truly Need

What is the biggest challenge that you're facing in your career right now? What don't you understand how to do? The answers to these questions will show you where you might need extra assistance right now. If you intend to hire staff or contract work out to another company or individual, you have to know up front what you expect from them. Deeper than that you should also know how the work they'll be doing for you ties into your divine vision (chapter 3). Questions to ask are:

- What skills must they have to truly support you right now?
- How do you expect them to give you that support?
- What emotions do you want to feel when you're interacting with them?
- What do you want your clients and customers to feel if they interact with this person/organization?

Once you are clear about the kind of support you need, close your eyes, take a few deep breaths and allow yourself to imagine that you have that support right now. Get in touch with the emotions want to experience when you're interacting with your support team. Imagine what it would look like/sound like/feel like. Then ask Spirit to bring those people to you right now. Also ask Spirit what to do now to get that support.

The next step is taking action. If you are posting job announcements or asking other people for referrals be honest and clear about the top qualities you're looking for in a new hire. Share why those qualities are important to the values of your company.

When you feel the energy of how you wish to be supported you will be able to compare that feeling to the energy of job applicants, coaches/mentors, systems, and others who may be able to support you. This allows you to feel if they are energetically aligned to your business or not.

When you meet with potential staff or mentors or when you're reviewing potential systems, ask yourself "does their energy match what I was looking for?" Think back to your intention and tune into your physical body. Does everything feel in harmony or is there discomfort somewhere?

Pay attention to any seemingly "random" ideas that come to your mind as potential job candidates are talking to you. Be honest about if that person is capable enough to support you in the way you need right now. If you really like a person but they don't have the skills to do what you need, do you honestly have the time and resources to get that person up to speed?

Remember that sometimes the person you resonate with the most is only resonating with you because both of you have a similar pain vibration. This will lead to conflict between the two of you later on. This is why focusing on whether or not the client resonates to your *divine vision* can be more accurate than tuning into if they resonate with you personally.

When you have a coach or you're part of an entrepreneur

group, it's important to make sure that you are actually receiving support. Some mentors and support groups are toxic instead of being helpful. In a healthy supportive relationship you should be treated with respect at all times and not belittled or made to feel like you could not succeed without that person. Also be weary of any person or group that spends time gossiping or blaming others for problems. Unstructured groups can quickly devolve into bitch sessions where everyone complains rather than helping members move forward.

Avoid spending time in networking or mastermind groups where the majority of people aren't really taking action to be successful. Even if they're pleasant to be around, if the majority of people in the group are still struggling with the same problems they were trying to overcome when they joined years ago, it's a sign that the group does not have the energy to help people move forward.

Be Clear and Honest With Expectations

When you have decided on hiring staff or investing in someone that can help you develop yourself or your business it is important that you are very clear with them about what your expectations are. It is also important that they are clear with you about what they need in order to meet those expectations. Never make assumptions about anything, no matter how obvious it may seem. Also pay attention to what your new hires are telling you. For example, if you need your assistant to work on your website and they say they don't feel comfortable doing that, believe them! If website support is a main function of the job you hired them to do, they may not be a good fit for you. Being honest about what you expect from your staff saves you time and money. Some people make the mistake of trying to make the job fit for a specific person as opposed to finding the right person for the job. This is connected to an "*I'm doing you a favor*" vibration which is discussed later in this chapter.

Over time you may realize that your needs are different than what you originally thought or you may have to invest more time and resources into the person you hired. If this happens, don't be discouraged. One of my coaches told me that it usually takes more time and more money than you originally planned to get your goals accomplished. I have found that to be true. Keep in mind that as your business changes and as you redefine your goals, people who were great support for you before the change will no longer be in your highest and best interest. Use your intuition to help you make decisions about when to invest more resources and when to walk away from systems or people that aren't truly being of service to you.

You Get What You Pay For

If you want the support of really talented people then expect to pay premium rates. Very rarely does a person suddenly experience massive success without investing significant time and resources into their career. People who have invested next to nothing in themselves will find that it takes years and years to reach the same level of success as a person who invested in better services sooner. This also applies to implementing systems in place that would streamline services and make tasks easier for everyone.

When you are faced with a big financial decision, before automatically saying "yes" or "no," tune in using your intuition. If you really would like to hire the person or buy the product or service, but you're concerned about the price, tune into how things would be if you and your business if you said yes. Trust the first impression you receive. Ask how things would be for you your business if you said no. Again, trust the first impression you receive.

Many people will receive an impression in their physical body as they tune in. Feeling heavy, sick, uncomfortable, or tired in your body is a strong "no" while feeling uplifted, supported, relieved, and happy is a strong "yes". For more information about how to understand what you're receiving intuitively, read the *Understand Your Intuition* section in chapter 2.

Hello Conflict

Even if you find the perfect support there will still be times when mistakes get made or when people disagree on the best way to help you move forward. This is especially true if you've hired new staff or if you've started a new project. It takes time for everyone's energy to synch together. The time it takes depends on the energy of each person involved and how clear your expectations are defined.

Depending on your personality, you may very uncomfortable with having disagreements. Conflict may be uncomfortable but it doesn't have to be negative. You can use your intuition to channel grace and understanding into the situation. To do this:

1. Take a moment before you speak to the other person and get clear on what you want the final outcome of the meeting to be, including how you want to feel afterward.
2. Focus on that feeling; imagine that your desired outcome already exists.
3. Say silently or out loud, "Spirit channel the energy into the situation that will give the highest and best resolution for everyone involved."

When you have to address conflict it is important to stay focused on wanting a resolution and not get caught up in the energy of complaining. Don't make assumptions about the other person (or people's) motive, especially if you didn't set clear boundaries and expectations up front. Instead, focus on facts, what you observed, and what you want the resolution to be. Really listen to other people's perspective. This allows your intuition to give you deeper insight about the situation.

Support Your Energy

As you work with your intuition you become more sensitive to the energy around you. This means that you will get better and better at understanding your intuition. It also means that you will be very aware of your pain. You will feel everything more strongly. When clients work with me I recommend that they work with other professionals who can help them release the pain of their emotional wounds and subconscious limiting beliefs in the easiest way. I use my intuition to know what types of energy clearing and healing will help them the most. Below is a list of different modalities that may help you. This list is not all-inclusive—there are thousands of healing modalities in the world. I've only included what I know has given my clients the best results. As you read through this list, notice if one or more items seem to stand out to you. That is a cue from your intuition that that service may be in your highest and best interest.

- Hypnotherapy – Hypnosis bypasses the conscious mind and goes straight to the subconscious. Hypnotists talk directly to the subconscious mind and give suggestions that can dissolve limiting beliefs and imprint your divine vision. There are many different types of hypnotherapists, some specialize in specific areas like stress management, weight loss, or even past life regression.
- Emotional Freedom Technique (EFT) – This is a very easy modality to learn yourself; it involves tapping on acupressure points on your body to scramble and dissolve the energy of limiting beliefs and emotional wounds. It is a very simple and powerful technique.
- The Emotion Code – Dr. Bradley Nelson is the author of a book called *The Emotion Code (How to Release Your Trapped Emotions for Abundant Health, Love, and Happiness)*. This book teaches how to release trapped emotional wounds from your body. There are practitioners all over the world who specialize in using this technique to help others clear trapped emotions. This can be done remotely or in person. Unlike some of the other modalities, you don't have to give much

detail about what you're trying to clear (unless it's needed and in most cases it isn't.)

- Energy healing – There are many different types of energy healers. Reiki is one of the most popular forms of energy healing but that is not the only one. Energy healing usually involves a person clearing your aura and chakra system. It may be hands on or hands off. A good energy healer can help reset your vibration and clear other people's energy and the energy of past life or ancestral lineage you may be carrying. Like hypnosis, some specialize in certain areas such as removing negative energy, heart healing, and more.

- Meditation circle – There is something very powerful about meditating with groups of people, especially if the meditation circle allows you to put in your own intentions and blessings for yourself and the world. The energy of the group can channel greater healing from Spirit into the world. This makes it easier to manifest what you desire and release what's been holding you back. There are many different types and styles of meditation. It may take a short while to find a group that you resonate with.

Be selective about who you allow to do any type of energy work on you. When you first meet a practitioner, tune into your physical body. When you're around them if you start feeling discomfort it is a sign that they are not a good fit for you, no matter how many other people love them.

Always remember that energy work is not a substitute for medical advice or treatment from medical professionals.

Subtle Energy Traps

As written above, having the right support can accelerate your success. Reasons why some people never seem to attract the right support or attract toxic support are tied to the pain of their subconscious limiting beliefs. Some common blocks preventing people from having supportive relationships are:

Trades

When some people realize they need support and see the price for what that support will cost, they may decide to enter into a trade. Instead of an exchange of money a person trades products or services for products and services from another. Trades can easily become an energy trap over time. Often times one person in the trade will feel like they are giving more product or service than what they are receiving.

For people who are struggling financially, getting into a trade reinforces the energy of not receiving money. If a person isn't paying you they may not see the value in what you're giving them. If you're dealing with a person who has low self-esteem and is undercharging for their own services a trade allows them to stay safe in the comfort zone of their pain. It will be harder for that person to take what you have to say seriously if you are coaching them or helping them move through challenges.

There are always exceptions to the rule. If you really feel a trade is in your highest and best interest, do it. Create a contract for the trade that sets a clear end date for the trade and outlines what is being traded so there are no misunderstandings.

Some people don't want to enter into a trade but they really want to work with the other person. It's the other person who can't afford their services. They may agree to accept products or services that they don't really want so they can 'help' the other person out. This leads to the subtle energy trap of:

I'm Doing You A Favor

Nearly every person I've worked with has had a moment when they hired a person on their staff or agreed to pay or trade for services from someone because they wanted to help the other person. They did this because the person was a friend or family member or because they liked the person and wanted to help them succeed. The underlying energy of why they hired that person was "I'm doing you a favor."

In almost all of these situations, this energy backfired. The person they hired didn't see them as a true boss; they actually resented being given work assignments and often did bare minimum. One of them actually told my client, "I'm doing *you* a favor!"

The underlying energy of "I'm doing you a favor" is connected to a block around receiving. Something within my clients didn't feel as though they deserved to be supported. Instead of finding true support my clients were paying to take care of people!

If you're not getting the level of service you expect from your staff or from an organization you hired, ask for clarity from Spirit about the current situation. Trust your true feelings around if it's time to find different support.

It is also important that you heal your relationship with receiving. Connecting with Spirit every day, sitting in the power of your energy will help you do this. The meditations in chapters 11 – 13 will also help.

If You Love Me You Would Support Me

As I wrote in the beginning of the chapter, most of my clients often feel alone on their career journey even if they have families and friends. This didn't mean that their families were unsupportive or dysfunctional. When I first discovered I was intuitive, I was excited and afraid. My friends and family were used to me being an accountant—normal. Suddenly I was a psychic who could talk to the dead—different. I was afraid of being judged if I told people and for many months I kept my intuition to myself.

Eventually I realized I wanted to start my own intuitive business. I couldn't keep what I was doing secret if I went professional. I got up enough courage to tell my mother and my best friend. My mother was afraid and didn't want me to put myself out there. She wanted me to just be an accountant and think before I made a decision to go professional. My best friend told me, "You know I'm a Christian and I don't believe in that stuff but if you do, I can respect that. I just don't want to talk about it."

Their responses weren't what I was hoping for. I immediately went into judging them. If they really loved me, they would be supportive of me 100%. They would trust and have faith in me. I seriously considered dropping my friend and avoiding my mother altogether. I distanced myself from both of them, which made me feel even more alone.

I found a group of people at a local metaphysical shop that met every weekend for a special meditation. I made friends with the people in the group who were very much into spirituality; they embraced me. I soon found that even though the people in the group were nice, they weren't a replacement for my best friend.

My best friend had my back, she had always been there for me and I had always been there for her. I could always be myself around her--up until I came out of the crystal closet anyway. I reached out to her and when we spoke it was like nothing had changed; she was happy to hear from me. She treated me the same as always—she didn't try to make me give up being intuitive and I didn't try to convince her my abilities were real. I realized she was sincere when she said that she respected me. More importantly, she loved me the same way. We became even closer—the realization that we could love each other through our differences and not judge each other was very powerful.

I still needed someone to talk to about my 'woo-woo' side; I made a point to surround myself with other people from the meditation circle and from the classes I attended who understood that part of me and could genuinely help me be a better intuitive and help my business succeed.

As I pursued my passion and started seeing clients, my mother changed her opinion. She even told me that she always supported my decision!

I share this personal example because many people expect their loved ones to support them in EVERY way, to be their EVERYTHING. While it is possible it is rare to have one person in your life who can support you in all ways. My mother and best friend didn't fully understand what I was doing and didn't understand how important my business was to me. If I had truly dropped my friend or my mother out of my life, I would have missed out on the loving relationships I really needed.

It's not necessary to wait for your loved ones to support you in order for you to purse your business goals. It's also not necessary for them to understand why what you're doing is important. Being resentful of loved ones in your life who don't 'get you' will only hold you back. Your focus can turn into proving yourself to them more than pursuing your dreams. Most people won't see your brilliance until you're very successful in what you do. It's not because they don't love you, it's because they genuinely don't understand. That said, if you have people in your life who belittle you or don't treat you with love or respect it might not be in your highest and best interest to have them in your life.

No Room For Error

If you supervise employees or hire support there will be times when those employees make mistakes or misunderstand your directions. Some of the managers and entrepreneurs I meet take the mistakes their employees make personally. Instead of viewing mistakes as a misunderstanding, they make assumptions that their employees are not serious about the job or that they're purposefully sabotaging the business. The way these bosses react is very passive aggressive. This means that instead of directly talking to an employee when a conflict arises, they make sarcastic comments that hint at what they're really upset about. They may also focus their attention on the employee rather than the conflict, attacking their employee's character rather than truly understanding what the conflict is and how to resolve it.

Extreme versions of this negative vibration will also cause bosses to throw tantrums or verbally attack their staff. The reason that this happens is that they honestly feel like each mistake someone makes is an attempt to destroy their business. Because they feel threatened they go on the attack.

These kind of bosses are usually very good at what they do and may have an extremely successful organization. However, they may have a constantly rotating staff. They create a toxic environment where most of their employees don't feel safe and become disillusioned. This toxicity spreads to other staffs, even those not supervised by the tyrannical boss.

If you are easily triggered when someone on your staff makes a mistake or if you're constantly hiring and firing staff you may have this issue. The first step to overcoming this energy is to accept your role in your experience. When you think someone is sabotaging your business or when you have a judgment of them, ask yourself, "is this belief coming from my pain or my brilliance?" It is also important to ask yourself why you are so upset when someone makes a mistake.

When you're the boss you are held to a higher level of standard. It is your job to be clear with your staff about what you expect them to do and how their work relates to the organization's mission. It's also important that you address any behavior that's in conflict with those goals right away with an honest and direct conversation.

When conflict arises it is best to take the position of "What can I do to help you succeed?" instead of an attitude of "why are you making my life miserable?" Employee mistakes can uncover where the organization has unclear procedures or procedures that aren't effective. Everyone makes mistakes. If you truly believe you've done everything in your power to help an employee succeed and they still aren't performing the tasks they need to perform, you may have to let them go. Ask Spirit for clear guidance about what to do in that situation.

If you are the employee working for a boss or with coworkers who behave this way, it's up to you to set very clear energetic boundaries by staying present and being mindful when other people's energy attempts to connect with you. The *Understand Your Intuition* section of chapter 2 will help you do this. It is also necessary for you to be honest about what you're willing to tolerate and what you aren't. Toxic work environments are very much like domestic abuse situations—employees may start feeling depending on the boss or the organization. They fear if they leave they might not find something else that pays as well or gives them the opportunities they need. They also may fear speaking up about the situation for fear of being ostracized or retaliated against. Constantly working in a high stress or fear filled environment affects your health and wellbeing. There is more than one path to the success you desire. You get to choose if you want that path to be supportive and loving or if that path is filled with strife and misery. Get clear about what you really want and use the five steps to manifest success (chapter 3) to help you get out of toxic situations.

CHAPTER 8
HATERS AND A#$HOLES AND DRAINS (OH MY!)

Ugh. That's the best way to describe the person when they walk through your door--whether they are a client, associate, frenemy, or family member; their very presence tires you. If you can move past the initial trigger you feel when you interact with a difficult person you will realize that difficult people are a good thing. They are the mirrors to the pain you are carrying in your subconscious limiting beliefs. By interacting with them you can find the limiting beliefs holding you back from living the life you want. Once you see those beliefs, you have the power to make changes and let go of that energy. A book that explains this concept in more detail is *The Four Agreements* by Don Miguel Ruiz.

It's important to note that just because someone may be mirroring a limiting belief you are carrying doesn't mean that they are excused from their behavior. You don't deserve to be victimized or disrespected.

The Myth of Energy Vampires
I am surprised at how many people routinely label others as

being "energy vampires". Energy vampires are difficult people who drain you of your energy, interacting with them can make you feel overwhelmed and exhausted in a very short amount of time. Spirit showed me early on that labeling someone an "energy vampire" is a way to blame someone else for how we feel. No one can drain our energy without our permission.

It is true that people who are in a tremendous amount of pain can take your energy. Most of the time they aren't doing this on purpose. What happens is that when you interact with them, you intuitively sense the pain in their energy. Something within you wants to make that person feel better. On a subconscious level you begin trading energy with that person because you want to help. You take on their negativity and they take your good vibrations.

If you're a person who always fixes things, the person your friends and family always go to when they need advice or to feel better, be on high alert. People who truly desire to help others are drained the most; they unknowingly take on negative energy because they want to heal it. Once you take on a person's negative energy they can actually form an energetic cord that connects to your vibration. This means that even when you're not around the person you are both still trading energy with each other.

Signs of being connected to someone else's energy include feeling "scattered," being unable to focus or concentrate, and having discomfort in your physical body. When a person first attempts to drain your energy you will receive an immediate impression in your physical body. The way that this feels is different for everyone. You can stop unauthorized energy trades by saying "no thank you" when you feel that energy attempting to connect to you. More information about this can be found in chapter 2 in the *Understand Your Intuition* section.

Setting boundaries is extremely important in stopping yourself from being drained. Remember, you automatically help people by doing what you love. Spirit channels healing energy *through* you into the lives of the people around you. You aren't supposed to give your own energy away to someone else. This means that it's not your job to rescue someone or to fix people. Sometimes, the best way to help others is to allow yourself to shine. This means you have to focus on what you want to experience and take actions that support your vision. As you become successful, you hold the energy of success for everyone around you.

Many of my clients who felt drained and taken advantage of weren't good at setting boundaries. They were undercharging for their services or giving their customers extra time or extra products for free. Their own actions were draining their energy. Once my clients took responsibility for their role in being drained, they were able to stop the cycle by making different decisions that supported their true desires.

Setting boundaries also applies to your personal life. This may mean that you support family and friends in finding a therapist or a coach that can really help them with their issues rather than listen to them continually complain. It may also mean that you do have to stop spending much time with them. Your intuition will help you make those decisions. Again, you'll *feel* it. When you find yourself feeling irritated or sick to your stomach or other feelings of discomfort, it's a sign from your intuition that the people you're around are not in your highest and best interest right now.

Like Attracts Like

On an energetic level, there are many different reasons why an entrepreneur may be attracted to a person who causes them to be irritated or distressed. Below are some of the underlying energies that create this attraction:

The "Prove It" Vibration

People caught in the "prove it" vibration spend an extraordinary amount of time trying to prove their expertise and value to others. They often attract difficult clients and other people that question every decision they make.

Another trap of the prove-it vibration is that entrepreneurs may actively pursue clients that just aren't that into them. They consistently reach out to people who they believe need their services even when those people aren't interested. They spend so much time trying to convince others to work with them that they start caring more about proving their worth more than being of service.

The energy of "prove it" comes from underlying insecurity. A person who spends time trying to prove their value to other people is really trying to prove their worth to themself.

I invite you to look at your business and even your personal life and ask yourself if you've been trying to prove your worth to someone. Where you are constantly trying to convince another person that you're right or that they should listen to what you have to say? What are you really trying to prove? Why do you want to prove it to those people?

When you notice you are trying to "prove it," say silently or out loud, "I surrender the need to prove myself. I love myself deeply and completely." The *Clear Your Energy* breathing exercise in chapter 13 will help you surrender this and more negative energies that you recognize.

Distraction

Over the years I noticed that many clients would suddenly have a major fight or get very upset with the people in their personal lives. This seemed to happen at the same time that they were starting to take a significant action in their business. Spirit showed me that this was a subtle defense mechanism.

My clients' were feeling discomfort as they moved outside of their comfort zone and took bigger actions in their career. The subtle energy of their fear was shifting their focus off of their business actions and onto being upset with everyone around them. The emotional pain my clients felt was real and intense but the cause of that pain wasn't from their family or friends. Their own fear was distracting them from making changes.

When you have to take an important action in your career, notice how you feel when you interact with others. If you find yourself annoyed or upset with someone ask yourself:

What am I afraid of doing or worried about in my career?

What do I need right now to feel supported?

When you bring your focus back to yourself and get in touch with your true feelings you will find the subtle fears and worries you are ready to release. Remember you can surrender emotions and beliefs that aren't serving you to Spirit. To learn how to surrender negativity read the *Who's Pain Is It Anyway* section in chapter 1.

The "Victim"

The victim vibration is deceptive. On the surface, people with this vibration look like true victims of circumstance. Bad things just seem to happen to them. They are very attached to talking about their problems and their problems are real.

A person with a strong victim vibration may have a subconscious limiting belief that the only way they can get love and affection is to be in crisis. Their energy then puts them in the wrong place at the wrong time to manifest this rule. If you yourself recognize this behavior, the *Clear Your Energy* breathing exercise in chapter 13 help you release that energy.

When a person with a victim vibration shows up, the worst thing you can do is feel sorry for them. Feeling sorry for another person only holds the vibration that the person is powerless. Instead of feeling sorry, pray. Praying for yourself or others is very powerful. The prayer I use for dealing with people in tremendous pain is: *Spirit, please give [NAME] whatever they need in their life right now to feel divinely loved, supported, and whole. Amen.*

This prayer works because you are holding a sacred space of love and power for another person.

The "Asshole"

Everyone one of us has an area of our lives where it feels like we keep facing the same challenges time and again. The energy of our pain can be so subtle that we don't even realize that we're the ones sabotaging our own success.

Looking closer at what bothers you about "assholes," the people who really annoy you, can lead you into discovering where you're still tolerating an asshole energy within yourself.

The more that you are aware of what you're truly feeling, thinking, and experiencing, the more you will start to see where your own limiting beliefs are being reflected back to you. Being present also means that you have the willingness to see the truth of a situation as it is without adding more to the story. What you add to the story comes from the pain you're carrying.

A client of mine came to a session very irritated. One of her customers was complaining about not being able to understand a bill she'd given him. She was convinced that her customer was just stalling on paying the invoice. When I asked why she was so upset she told me that once again she had a customer who wasn't respecting her work and the value of what she was providing.

"People just don't even realize how much goes into this," she said. "They don't treat this like a real business."

I asked, "Where in your life do you feel you're acting the same way, where you don't see what you do as being a 'real' business?"

She took a deep breath and admitted she'd been feeling a *little* that way about herself—she didn't feel confident in everything she was doing. She still didn't have a professional office space or a core team that could help her do all of the tasks she needed assistance with. When we talked through it, her irritation lifted and we began work on the core limiting belief: that *she* didn't feel like she had a real business.

This is an example of how being present led to a breakthrough in energy. "A customer questioned the invoice" was the only truth of the situation. My client added to the story by assuming the customer was questioning the invoice because he didn't see her as having a real business. In reality my client was projecting her limiting belief on him.

Once you notice your limiting beliefs in action you can make different decisions and take different actions from the energy of your brilliance instead of your pain. Again, this requires the courage to be present and honest with what you're feeling, even when you are experiencing painful moments.

If you are irritated by partners, clients, or other people that you don't care for, take notice of what's really irritating you. Questions to ask yourself are:

- Why does this bother me so much?
- What's being reflected back to me?
- Where in my life am I acting the same as this difficult person?

Haters

Haters are usually a sign that you're doing something right. It may not feel comfortable when someone says something mean about you or your motives but know that they are only acting that way because your energy was so strong that it nudged a subconscious limiting belief inside of them. If deep down they have a belief that "no one in my industry makes money" and they hear successful you're doing, they will find themselves feeling threatened. Their mind might give them all sorts of reasons why you were able to make money and they weren't. Most of their reasons will make you look like the 'bad guy.'

On an energetic level when someone is hating on you, they are sending you energy. If you stay focused on what you want to accomplish, the energy that was sent to you will reset from negative to positive and amplify your manifestation power. This is why hated celebrities continue to flourish in spite of thousands of people disliking them—they are being energetically fed by the masses.

A hater can't negatively impact your energy unless you agree with what they're saying. Remember, you may not think you agree but on a subconscious level, you might have emotional wound that their comment hooks into. You know you an emotional wound or subconscious limiting belief if you find yourself getting upset by what someone else has said or written about you. If you focus on that person or what was written then a cord gets created between you and the hater and you start feeding that person your energy. This will cause you to feel tired and overwhelmed. Clear your energy and keep returning to your divine brilliance to break any toxic energetic connections. The meditations in chapters 11 – 13 will all help you do this.

When you start going to the next level of success in your business, people in your close circle of friends and family may also suddenly start having 'hater' tendencies, saying rude things to you, getting upset with you, or even accusing you of doing things that you aren't doing. This happens as you stand in the power of your soul brilliance.

As your energy becomes clear it will start raising and clearing the energy of the people around you. This means they will become more sensitive to their own energy and really start noticing their own limiting beliefs. If they are unwilling to take responsibility for their happiness they will project their limiting beliefs onto you. What they accuse you of doing is what they see in themselves. Most people won't know that they're doing this. All they'll know is that when you're around they suddenly don't feel good about themselves.

Over time your real friends and true supporters will grow closer to you while other people drift away. The way to deal with haters is to turn your focus back to yourself and what you want to do. The exception to that rule is if the hater is threatening you or if you are being defamed.

Report threats of violence or stalking to the police. At this time, there may not be legislation to protect you from online threats but it is important to document what you are experiencing.

If a hater is defaming you or your business, which means that they are lying about you in a way that would cause you or your business harm, consult an attorney to see how to properly handle the situation. Document what was said or posted right away.

CHAPTER 9
SPECIAL CONSIDERATIONS FOR PSYCHICS, MEDIUMS, AND HEALERS

Many psychics, mediums, and healers struggle with the same limiting mindset beliefs that are tied to a wounded healer or martyr vibration. This vibration is not truly divine brilliance but an aspect of pain. When a psychic, medium, or healer is consciously in tune with Spirit, they manifest profound healing and transformation for themselves as well as their clients.

As I transitioned from working as a financial analyst for the federal government into becoming a professional intuitive, I met many other psychics and mediums that were brilliant in their work but were struggling to make a consistent income. What bothered me was that many of these mediums *expected* that they weren't going to make a lot of money. I also witnessed respected leaders in the industry tell healers to expect other forms of suffering, saying things like:

- The energy of spirit is hard on the body so mediums (and other energy healers) will get sick more often
- Psychics who are serious about the work won't find a

romantic soulmate on earth because their work is too important to settle down

- Heart-centered psychics don't charge much for readings because they care about being of service

When I heard these things it didn't make sense to me. I also began to question if I was really a good intuitive--I was making money and I hardly ever got sick. I hadn't found a romantic soulmate. Did that make me miserable enough to be a 'good' healer? Or should I be experiencing more pain?

One day while I was meditating I had a vision of a large box wrapped in shiny paper with a big red bow on top. This was a message from Spirit, showing me a gift. The gift moved closer to me so I could clearly see the words stamped on the side. Written in capital letters was "SUFFERING NOT INCLUDED." With the vision came a clear understanding from spirit: being gifted does not mean you have to suffer. We choose that on our own.

I began noticing that as I let go of other people's expectations that mediums had to suffer, my business flourished. My healing gifts also increased—as I continued my intuitive coaching practice my clients started seeing leaps of progress within weeks instead of months or years. I

After helping my clients (and myself) shift from struggling to experiencing miracles I know without a doubt that psychics, mediums, and other energy healers are the people most able to create the life that they want in the easiest way possible. This is because they have a conscious connection to Spirit. However, many of these healers don't fully understand their gift. They get caught up in the expectation that life is supposed to be hard and they end up manifesting someone else's limiting beliefs.

The stronger you are in your gift the more easily you can manifest your dream life. If you are experiencing constant feelings of overwhelm, sickness, or financial struggle *you* are choosing to manifest from your pain instead of manifesting from your brilliance.

What would you do if you could be rich? If you got to be

100% healthy all of the time? What bigger contributions to the world could you make if you had the resources to do it? What would you create? How many people could you reach? These types of questions can help you snap back into the vibration of your brilliance rather than staying in the limitations of your pain vibration.

The previous chapters in this book, especially chapters 1 - 5 will help you uncover where and why you are manifesting from pain and give you the tools to accept your blessings from Spirit. I also strongly recommend reading the book *Psychic Navigator* by John Holland.

Below are other important tools that are specifically geared to helping my brothers and sisters in the 'woo-woo' community overcome the unique challenges of being gifted.

I will be using the words "psychic," "medium," and "healer" interchangeably in this chapter so where you see one of those terms please know that I am referring to all members of the spiritual community.

Spirit Slaves vs Spirit Partners

You are always 100% connected to Spirit; you're spirit, and the energy of the Divine. This is different than linking to other energies outside of you such as perceiving dead people or living people's energy. Some people who have strong intuition or psychic ability find themselves wide open to random energies in their daily life. They make the mistake of feeling as though they have to be open to the spirit world all the time. This leads to feeling constantly overwhelmed or unwilling to be present.

You are not meant to be 'wide open' to random energy all of the time. You get to decide when and how you want to use your gift. This means that if you're a psychic and you'd rather use your gifts to help investment bankers know how to invest versus helping someone find their soulmate, honor your feelings. This also means that as a medium you should not be seeing dead people at all hours of the day or night. You're allowed to live your life and do what you want to do. You get to tell the spirit world how you want to work and when your office hours are. This doesn't make you less open to Spirit or make you come from a place of ego. Spirit wants to partner with you, not have you be a slave.

A person in the "slave to Spirit" vibration may go between extreme feelings of gratitude and resentment. They will feel like they *have* to do things they don't want to do in order to please Spirit. When they are actually using their gifts to help others they feel amazing gratitude and love because they are consciously connecting with Spirit. They will start feeling resentment at not making money or continually having to struggle in some other way. If you tell Spirit what you like and how you want to work, Spirit will honor your way. This means you have to be clear about everything you'd like to experience, including what kind of service you want to give, who you want to serve, what you would like to receive for your services, etc..

Some healers feel like they should just be open and not set any expectations. Their rationale is that if they are too specific about what they want they will limit Spirit from sending them something even better. This is not true. Being specific about what you like is part of your natural gift of discernment. Remember, your true desires are connected to your soul purpose. Honoring what truly makes you feel good and letting go of what truly doesn't resonate with you is part of honoring your soul experience. Not making decisions is you giving up your power and ignoring your soul.

In addition, a person who isn't clear about what they want will manifest from the energy that they're in instead of the energy they want to be in. This means you may manifest reality from your pain instead of your brilliance.

Healing Tools For Empaths

As written above no person is supposed to be open 24/7 to the random energies of the spirit world. Some people have difficulty knowing how to shut down their gift because they are extremely empathic. An empathic person has a great sensitivity to the energy around them. This sensitivity empowers them to be more intuitive and more connected to Spirit. However, empaths can be easily overwhelmed by the energy of other places, situations, and people. Symptoms of this include feeling drained, constantly attracting difficult people or situations, or having frequent moments of self-doubt, fear, or confusion.

If you can relate to those feelings, you are probably empathic. Here are tools that can help you set proper energetic boundaries so you get less of the energy you don't want. This will empower you to better understand your own intuition:

1. **Take Care Of Your Body**

   Eat healthy, exercise, and get plenty of rest. If you're tired or feeling bad it will be easier to get overwhelmed by energy.

2. **Stay Present**

   Be mindful of how you're feeling physically, emotionally, and mentally. When you're present you will be able to easily know when someone else's energy is affecting you.

3. **Set Proper Boundaries (Energetic)**

   Visualize a gold circle of light that completely surrounds you. Set the intention that this circle of light only attracts energies that are in your highest and best interest and repels energies that aren't. You can even set the intention that your Spirit Helpers such as guides and angels are reinforcing your sacred circle of light. Periodically throughout the day, re-visualize this circle around you.

4. **Set Proper Boundaries (Physical)**

   In your daily life, be sure that you are setting boundaries with people. This means saying 'no' to people and distancing yourself from those people or situations that are constantly draining you if possible.

5. **Ask Spirit For Help**

   Throughout the day if you encounter negative energies, pray for extra assistance from Spirit. If you have a strong resonance with angels, spirit guides, or ascended masters, ask those beings to keep your energy clear and free of all negativity. You can also ask for extra love and healing light.

6. **Ground Your Energy Daily**

   Ground your energy by exercising, sitting or laying on earth, hugging a tree or taking a hot bath with Epsom salts. For those sensitive to energy, grounding yourself with physical actions can be more effective than meditating.

7. **Use Tools**

   There are crystals (such as Labradorite), essential oils (such as Frankincense, Vetiver, Lavender, and Sage), sound healing with crystal bowls or even listening to your favorite music that can help keep your energy balanced and clear. However, tools work best when you are following the other steps above.

Daily meditation will help you understand your energy so that you easily recognize any energy that comes into your energy field that's not in your highest and best interest. If you use meditation and you're empathic, be sure the technique that you're using has a strong grounding exercise. Meditations that clear the chakras or have you get in touch with your physical body are examples of grounding meditations.

In addition, at the start of every day it is best to make sure that you are protecting your energy, which is just another way of setting boundaries about what you want to experience. The *Check In* breathing exercise in chapter 11 will help you tune into your own energy so you can release any energy that isn't serving you and will show you how to create a protective light around your energy.

Seriously, Get Grounded

As written above, healers have to make sure they are very grounded in the world. Being ungrounded can feel really great—the reason is that your spiritual energy is more outside of your body than in. This causes you to not be in touch with physical or emotional pain and discomfort. A person who isn't grounded has a hard time concentrating. Their thoughts are all over the place and they suddenly don't know how to make a decision.

Many people who are naturally sensitive to energy and are extremely intuitive will find that they can easily check out of their bodies. It is not healthy to spend long periods of time ungrounded, it makes it harder to live your daily life because you're not fully present with what you're experiencing on earth. Being ungrounded will also allow energies that aren't in your highest and best interest to connect to your vibration.

The easiest way to get grounded is to breathe and become present with how you feel in your physical body. You can also command, "All of my energy back in my body right now." Saying the word "reset" will also help to shift your energy wherever it needs to go within you.

You can ground your energy by exercising, sitting or lying on earth, hugging a tree or taking a hot bath with Epsom salts. For those who are very sensitive to energy, grounding yourself with physical actions can be more effective than meditating.

The more that you are able to ground the energy of spirit into your conscious awareness, the faster you can experience miracles.

It's Not Me, It's Spirit

Famous medium Lisa Williams once shared that there are still many mediums who operate from the negative part of ego where they don't acknowledge their role in mediumship. For example, when someone thanks the medium for a reading the medium says things like, "it's not me, it's Spirit" or "I didn't really do anything, it's all Spirit." Lisa saw this as the medium not honoring themselves. At the time she spoke, I was offender #1 of doing this. Whenever someone gave me a compliment for a reading, I took no credit for it. As I thought about why I felt the need to deflect compliments, I realized I had guilt around receiving *anything* for doing my spiritual work. Receiving a compliment made me feel like I was taking something away from Spirit and that I was getting something I wasn't supposed to have.

It is true that if you're a healer Spirit is working through you. It's also true that if you didn't show up for your client, Spirit wouldn't have had that opportunity to connect. When you're standing alone on a stage with a crowded room of people staring back at you, YOU are choosing to be brave. When you are spending countless hours perfecting your craft by going to classes, workshops, summits, etc., YOU are choosing to show up and invest your time, money, and other resources to honor Spirit in the best way. With every client you see and every class you teach, you are putting yourself at risk of receiving criticism and judgment from others because you are dedicated to being of service.

You've got to have crystal balls to work with Spirit. This isn't to be taken lightly. Not many people can do it. Honor your role in the process. If you don't, neither will other people. To many people you encounter you're the expert in your field. If you say you're not important, your clients and potential clients will believe you. Constantly deflecting compliments isn't a sign that you're humble; it's a subtle form of self-rejection, a feeling of "I'm not good enough to receive."

When you repeatedly say, "It's not me" or "I'm not doing anything" you are creating a powerful mantra. This can affect your subconscious mind by giving you the belief that you really aren't doing anything—which can make it harder for you to trust yourself in the way you need to trust to go further in your work.

A psychic friend of mine told me how she once gave an intense group reading and healing for several of her clients. One of the participants in the group thanked her for the experience, saying it was life changing. Another woman in the group quickly interrupted the person giving thanks with "you don't have to thank her, it's really Spirit." This caught my psychic friend off guard—she had put a lot of energy and effort into making sure everyone had a great experience. She was annoyed that someone was suggesting that she be un-thanked. Until she realized that the woman who spoke up was just repeating what she herself often said!

A client who is just trying to acknowledge your role in their healing journey isn't trying to worship you or detract from Spirit. If you find yourself deflecting compliments, really ask yourself why that is. Do you truly believe that what you're doing is valuable? Do you believe you should be paid for it? If you can't take a blessing as simple as a compliment, how do you expect to receive other blessings from the universe?

Ego Games

Our ego is just our individuality, the unique mental and emotional traits that make us who we are. Where ego can cause conflict is when a person attempts to believe in their ego more than their spirit. This means, really believing their thoughts and emotions above their intuition. Our subconscious limiting beliefs and emotional wounds also reside in the ego. When we believe what our thoughts and emotions are telling us, we experience reality based on those limitations. When most people say 'ego' they're usually referring to the part of the ego that causes people to act arrogant, selfish, mean-spirited, or not very enlightened.

I meet many healers who are so worried about coming from this negative aspect of ego that they minimize their skills and abilities. They are highly critical of themselves and dismiss their successes as being 'flukes' or 'getting lucky.' They are constantly looking for someone or something else to give them validation that they're heart-centered. This can lead to healers needing to receive constant approval from other people. It can also lead to psychics not going professional when they are truly ready. It almost always leads to mediums undercharging for their services—this is because they don't want to see the value in themselves.

These types of healers aren't just looking for approval from clients; they seek validation from other healers in their industry. They may set their prices according to what another person is doing or offer services just like someone else. They want others to believe that they're *good people*.

When a psychic is trying hard to prove that they're not coming from ego, they also have a tendency to talk negatively about themselves or other people in the industry. When they talk negatively about themselves, they are looking for someone else to step in and disagree, telling them how good they really are. Again, this isn't something that someone does with conscious awareness; they are being triggered by their subconscious mind.

When a healer continually gossips and talks negatively about other people it is usually because something those other people are doing is conflicting with a limiting belief that the healer has. For example, I was at an expo where one healer came up to me and said, *"Can you believe that psychic is charging that much for a reading?! Don't they know its Albuquerque, not California?"*

The two limiting beliefs that were being triggered in the healer were: 1) It's not okay to make a lot of money doing spiritual work and 2) people in Albuquerque don't pay much for spiritual services. When the healer saw people—Albuquerque people—paying to get readings from the psychic, he was triggered even more and continued to complain. He was looking for me to agree with him, to reinforce his belief that it wasn't okay to charge above a certain price for readings. By the end of the day, the psychic with the high prices ended up having the most clients of the day while the complaining healer had given away free healing services and had no paying clients.

Negative ego vibrations operate in a very subtle way. Some mediums will suddenly find themselves in a confrontation or heated disagreement with clients, colleagues, friends, or even family. The conflict will really trigger the medium—they will want to argue and prove to those people that they're *right*. The medium is triggered because the other person is reflecting back how the medium truly feels about themselves.

This doesn't mean that every disagreement you get into is caused by your subconscious limiting beliefs. It is only when you feel the emotional charge of anger, resentment, sadness, or another painful emotion that you know you are facing a belief that you are holding within yourself.

The way out of constantly worrying about your ego is to keep recognizing when you are manifesting from your ego pain versus your Divine brilliance. You don't have to put yourself down or minimize your accomplishments to keep your ego in check. You only have to accept yourself as you are and be honest about what you want to receive and experience in your life. The meditations in chapters 11 – 13 will help you keep your energy clear.

A Healthy Medium

For those people who are concerned about staying healthy as they do their spiritual work, nothing can replace a healthy diet and exercise. Any person in a career where they are sitting for long periods of time every day, most days of the week, is at risk of having poor health if they don't do eat right or move around.

When it comes to working with energy, it is important to continually keep yourself clear by grounding your energy and resetting your vibration through some form of meditation or yoga. Intense physical exercise is also good for releasing pent up energy.

CHAPTER 10
SUPPORT FOR YOUR UNIQUE SITUATION

I trust that by reading through this book you have a better understanding of how intuition and energy works and how you might use your intuitive ability to go to the next level of success in your career. Reading through the chapters may have given you deeper insight about how to improve your success but you may also have unique situations that don't quite fit some of the scenarios in the book.

There's no easy way to get support from one book. If you realize that you would like more support in reaching your business and career goals, contact me. I work one-on-one with clients from a variety of industries who have unique challenges and goals.

E-mail me at candice.intuitive@gmail.com and we can set up an appointment to talk about how I can be of service to you in your unique situation. I am available to do private intuitive readings and mediumship readings.

If you're interested in developing your intuition I teach a variety of intuitive development workshops throughout the year, including intuition for career success, to help you understand and strengthen your abilities. I also mentor a very small number of people each year who are interested in becoming professional intuitives or intuitive coaches like me. Information about my upcoming workshops events as well as testimonials from clients and students can be found on my website: candicethomasintutive.com.

While visiting my website be sure to join my mailing list to learn about upcoming webinars, live workshops, and coaching programs where you can receive more intuitive tools to manifest success and receive guidance.

The best way to develop your intuition is to practice. Because everyone's intuitive gifts are unique, you won't know how your intuition 'talks' to you until practice using it. It's also important to note that there aren't really 'rules' about the best way to expand your intuition. You don't have to give up meat or rap music in order to connect with Spirit.

The best books that will help you understand more about energy and your intuition are:
- *Psychic Navigator* by John Holland
- *Psychic Intelligence* by Terry & Linda Jamison
- *The Four Agreements* by Don Miguel Ruiz

The next chapters are meditations and breathing exercises so you can get in direct touch with Spirit. Write down what you experience as you do the meditations and breathing exercises so you remember what insights and impressions you receive.

Remember, you have the power to create the life you desire right now. All you have to do is listen to your divine brilliance and act on what you receive. Thank you reading and thank you for allowing me to be part of your journey.

Blessings,

Candice

CHAPTER 11
BREATHING EXERCISE: CHECK IN

This breathing exercise will help you check in with your energy so you become present with how you're truly feeling and what's affecting your energy. When you check in with yourself you open yourself up to your divine brilliance and are better able to understand your intuition. You are also able to release any energy that's not in your highest and best interest that you may have picked up from people or situations around you.

Get into a comfortable position and take deep breaths into your body. As you take those deep breaths get present with how your body feels.

Do you notice any tension or stiffness, discomfort or pain in your body? If so, imagine that you are breathing into those areas; sense your joints and muscles relaxing, loosening up, letting go of whatever doesn't serve you.

As you do this, you might be aware of different sensations, such as getting cooler, getting warmer, buzzing or tingling. Just be present with this experience and go deeper into your awareness.

Focus on your emotions. What emotions are strongest in you now? Keeping in mind you may be aware of more than one emotion. As you tune into those emotions, see if you can tell where are they in your physical body. Trust your first impression. For example, you might feel anxiety in your chest. You might feel sadness in your chest or even joy around you. What does that emotion feel like physically? How big is it? Is it moving?

Imagine that with the power of your breath you are breathing into the emotional energy. Your breath is dissolving any emotions that are not serving you, any emotions you are ready to release. Your breath balances your emotional body, aligning your emotions with the physical. All you have to do is breathe. And go further into your awareness.

Moving into your mental energy, notice what thoughts, images, or memories are coming to mind. See if you can stay in the role of just observing those thoughts as they come and go. With every breath you take imagine those thoughts loosening, allowing you to be more present and focus on your breath. Every breath releases the thoughts that aren't serving you, balancing your mental energy with your emotional and physical energies.

Go deeper now into your actual energy field. Imagine that your energy is a strong beam of light. Where is your energy right now? Is it balled up tightly around your head and shoulders? Is it off to one side of you? Is it scattered all over the place? Trust your first impression.

Say silently or out loud, "All of my energy back in my body right now." Imagine any part of your energy that has been scattered or disconnected from you easily and harmoniously reintegrating with the rest of your energy system. As you do this you might pick up on discomfort again in your physical body. With every breath you take, just imagine that that energy of discomfort or pain is being dissolved. Every breath out releases that discomfort down through your body, down through your feet, and into the earth for healing.

Say silently or out loud, "I reset my energy right now." Imagine your light filling you from head to toe within your body, becoming perfectly balanced. Sense your light centering within you, moving down from the top of your head to your toes, until you are perfectly glowing from the inside out with your light.

Notice how quickly and easily you're able to release energy that no longer serves you. All you have to do is breathe. Sit as long as you like feeling the power of your spirit.

CHAPTER 12
MEDITATION: YOUR DIVINE VISION

This guided meditation will help you experience the energy of your soul purpose and divine vision. Once you connect with these energies you will be able to experience the power of your brilliance and release the energy of your pain. Because this is a guided meditation it is best to record yourself speaking and listening to it rather than trying to read and meditate at the same time. To get the most out of this exercise be sure you have read chapters 1 - 3 and are clear about what you want to experience. A pre-recorded audio of this mediation is available. Visit candicethomasintuitive.com for more information.

EXPERIENCE YOUR DIVINE VISION
Take a few deep breaths and feel your energy, meaning just allow yourself to observe how you feel in your physical body. Breathe in through your nose and out through your mouth. Focus on your breath as the air travels in through your nostrils and down your lungs, feel your chest expand with air and contract as your breath travels back up through your lungs and out of your mouth. Really become present with how it feels to breathe. Allow your

eyes to close if they're not closed already.

Set the intention that your vibration is lifting and raising. This just means that you're becoming more sensitive and more perceptive to your own spirit, your own soul, your higher self. We invite all of your spirit helpers to be with you at this time. Only those beings in your highest and best interest: your angels and archangels, spirit guides, and ascended masters, and all other beings who can help you the most in this moment. These beings are helping you the hold sacred space around you. With them, you lift and raise your vibration even higher.

We ask that these beings step even closer to you in frequency and vibration, in the highest and best way. As they step closer, we invite your higher self to connect with you in a more conscious way. We invite your mind to merge with your higher mind right now. Think about what you would like to accomplish in your career. Who would you like to be of service to? How are you helping them? Where are traveling to be of service? What are you saying? What do you see? Use your imagination to really see this, hear this, feel this.

As you think about who you're serving imagine the love and support that you're receiving from them, their gratitude and thankfulness. What are your emotions as you realize that you're doing everything you've dreamed of?

Surrendering now to your higher self and your soul's perspective we ask that your soul shows you more of what you're meant to experience. Allow your soul to give you the impression or the feeling of your real clients, your real customers, who you're really going to be working with, what you're really meant to be doing to help them. It may come to you as a knowing. or a feeling. Or you may hear words or see an image. Trust what you perceive.

Staying with your Divine Vision, look around you. Who's with you? Who's part of your team? Are you speaking from world stages? Are you being interviewed? Are you in magazines? Have you created a larger company? Just trust what you experience. Trust what rolls into your awareness.

What other ways are you helping people or other beings? How does that make you feel?   Remember to breathe. Every breath you take intensifies the vibration, the energy of your Divine spirit.

Going further into your vision, become present with what you are receiving.   Where are you traveling? Where do you live? What does your home look like? What do you have? Do you own a jet? What other toys are you aware of? Who are you meeting? What are you hearing? What are you seeing? What do you know? How does it feel to have all of these abundant blessings?   Trust your first impression, and if you notice discomfort around what's happening, that's okay, bring your focus and awareness back to the divine center, your truth, letting go of limitations.   Bring your focus back to all the service that you're providing to receive all of these blessings. Sense how easy it is to do what you love in the way that you love to do it.

Ask spirit to give you the idea, the knowledge of what you are creating.   As you fulfill your soul purpose and achieve your dreams, what lessons have you learned? Who are you sharing your story with? Who are you influencing?

Take a deep breath and continue experiencing this vibration. In this space, imagine your career or business as its own separate light, as its own separate energy. As you tune in to this energy notice if it feels aligned with your divine vision. Does it make you soar or does it seem to drag or pull on your energy?

At this moment set the intention that the energy of your

business or career is being reset and aligned with your true soul purpose and soul intention right now. Sense the energy of your divine brilliance channeling through you, through your vibration, into the heart of your career, empowering your business.

Sense all of your perfect clients and opportunities being attracted to your light right now, those clients who truly love, respect, and support what you do, customers who are ready, able, and happy to pay your desired rates. Mentors and partners who are ready, able, and happy to support you in your goals. Sense how easy it is to connect with them in your way. Sense how appreciative they are, the gratitude they have of finding you. Sense the level of service that you're providing them, how you're truly able to help them move forward right now.

As you do this you might already be aware that you are becoming a beacon for opportunities, miracles, and blessings that you didn't even realize were possible. This process is opening you to the grace and brilliance of your divine spirit and the divine itself. This energy fills you from head to toe, aligning your energy centers and all of the cells in your body, all the way down to a DNA level. From this moment forward, everything you see, everything you hear, everything you say, everything you feel, and every action you take will move you forward in alignment with your divine vision whether you are consciously aware of it or not.

Be present with this energy and how you feel.

Imagine your energy like a bright light. That light connects all the way down through your feet into the center of the earth, as you connect with the center of the earth imagine your energy is being grounded in the world. This means that you have the ability to manifest your vision easily and completely in the world.

We ask from your soul's perspective, "what is in my highest and best interest to release from my life right now?" Trust what comes to your awareness. "What is in my highest and best interest to do right now?" and "What do I do now to move my career forward in the highest and best way?" Trust what comes to your awareness.

Breathe. Be present with this experience.

If there's anything you would like assistance with or if you need extra guidance, ask Spirit now. For example, "who do I reach out to?" "What's in my highest and best interest to let go of?" Trust what comes to your awareness. Keep in mind you may only receive one word or a feeling or a knowing. Be present with your first impression without judging yourself.

It is now almost time to come out of this meditation. We thank your higher self and your spirit helpers for their assistance. Know that your energy is being reset to the perfect level right now that will allow you to continue your day-to-day tasks. If you'd like you can stay in this sacred space connected with your divine brilliance. Each time you connect with Spirit in this way you expand your emotional, mental, and physical awareness, so that you can easily see, feel, hear, know, even taste and smell the guidance from your higher self.

Take a few more deep breaths and when you're ready, slowly and gently open your eyes.

CHAPTER 13
BREATHING EXERCISE: CLEAR YOUR ENERGY

This breathing exercise is about clearing your energy and releasing subconscious limiting beliefs and emotional wounds. If you are struggling with physical, mental, or emotional pain, you can surrender that energy to Spirit using this meditation. Please note that this exercise is not a substitute for seeing a medical professional if you have health concerns, nor is it a substitute for medical instructions you received from a medical professional.

CLEAR YOUR ENERGY

Take a few deep breaths.

Silently or out loud say, "I invite those beings who are in my highest and best interest who can help me the most with clearing my energy to connect with me right now. Spirit give me whatever I need to feel whole, loved, and divinely supported right now. Spirit take away all energies from all layers of my being that are not in my highest and best interest right now. Dissolve cords, connections, and attachments to that energy completely right now."

You can silently or out loud ask for anything specific you desire. If you want Spirit to give you something specific, add 'right now' and 'easily' to the end. For example, "Please Spirit, bring me my perfect clients easily right now." or "Please Spirit, completely and easily heal this situation right now."

Surrender any emotions or feelings you've been struggling with by saying, "I surrender [name the emotion or feeling.]" For example, "I surrender jealousy. I surrender feeling like I'm not enough." If you're unsure you can always say, "I surrender whatever I need to surrender to be the person I'm meant to be."

Sit for a moment in the feeling of Spirit, remembering to keep taking deep breaths.

All you have to do is feel your energy. This doesn't mean you have to think about it, just feel it. Cry if you need to; be angry if that's what comes up. You may even recall past events from your life that happened years ago. Just be present with how you feel and what you experience.

If you are numb to your feelings it may take a few times before you notice a difference in energy. Trust in the process.

NOTES

_____

_____

_____

_____

_____

_____

_____

_____

_____

_____

_____

_____

_____

_____

_____

_____

_____

_____

ABOUT THE AUTHOR

Candice Thomas had been a supervisor and financial analyst in a federal government agency for over 10 years when her intuitive and mediumship gifts awakened. The experience led her on a path to understand the nature of intuition, Spirit, and soul purpose. As she developed her intuitive abilities she discovered that she could 'tune in' to other people's soul mission and see their highest potential. At the same time she realized that the people around her were also intuitive, whether they realized it or not. Spirit began guiding her to help people use their intuitive abilities to manifest the life they desired.

Candice now combines her leadership, coaching, and intuitive abilities to help clients unlock their own intuition and use their gifts on purpose to manifest their true desires. Several of her clients have experienced significant increases in income, been featured in national publications, created unique and innovative programs in their industry, and have developed their own ability to receive and understand intuitive guidance from Spirit.

For more information about Candice visit candicethomasintuitive.com

Manufactured by Amazon.ca
Bolton, ON

13833353R00085